'Better than most, I knew that she was hurting about her lost love, so I hadn't been very surprised when she took up with someone else that summer. She had earned a break, and the relationship with Dodi Fayed . . . might have been the perfect summer fling. But if it had, indeed, been designed to inspire another's jealousy, I doubt that the tactic worked. If anything, he would have been horrified by the reminder of the depth of public interest in anything she said or did, or anywhere she went, and with whom. . . .'
—from *Diana: The Secret Years*

DIANA

The Secret Years

Simone Simmons
with Susan Hill

BALLANTINE BOOKS • NEW YORK

A Ballantine Book
Published by The Ballantine Publishing Group
Copyright © 1998 by Simone Simmons

www.randomhouse.com/BB/

Library of Congress Catalog Card Number: 99-90362

ISBN 0-345-43590-7

Manufactured in the United States of America

First Hardcover Edition: November 1998
First Mass Market Edition: August 1999

10   9   8   7   6   5   4   3   2   1

Contents

Acknowledgements

With many thanks to the following: my friends David Helsten, RMT and Gillian Garrow for all their support and encouragement; Morris Power, the epitome of humanitarianism, for telling me of life's raw realities; Susan Hill for her hard work; Tony Clayman, my agent, for listening to my worries; Michael O'Mara, my publisher, whose gentle pushing and encouragement have been very comforting. I would also like to thank Martin Bristow, Toby Buchan, Emma Haynes and Andrew Morton.

Finally, I thank my close family—Frances, Rachel, Juliette and Russel, Gideon, Mattea and Jemina—for being there, and my cats, who offer total, unconditional love.

Simone Simmons
September 1998

I dedicate this book to the ideals for the future of the late Diana, Princess of Wales: global peace, and an end to human suffering.

Preface

Diana asked me to write this book.

It was in February 1997. She was sprawled on one of the sofas in her private sitting room at Kensington Palace and I had adopted my customary and comfortable place on the floor, propped up on the large stuffed fake hippopotamus in front of the hearth. We had been laughing like drains as she recounted another little story about her life—the real thing, her version—not the tabloids' or Buckingham Palace's. Yet again there had been a TV programme that evening which had got things all wrong. She dabbed at her eyes with a Kleenex, laughed again and ordered me, one day, to write a book and 'tell it like it is'.

'They'll say I'm the nutty princess and that you're the nutty psychic,' she warned, quite cheerfully, 'but I want you to tell the truth. It'll be about time.'

The *Daily Mail* journalist Richard Kay, one of her other close friends, was with us as we watched the documentary. Diana had been particularly amused during the programme by the neat turn of her butler Paul Burrell's calves, for he had been filmed wearing livery during his days as a footman at Buckingham Palace. But her request—indeed, demand—for truth from us was utterly serious.

She was so tired of the misquotes, the misunderstandings and the misjudgements. That afternoon she was quite entertained by allusions in the programme to her caprices, her extravagances and sulks. Previously, such reports had often angered her, but by then she had become strong enough to laugh sometimes, and to appoint me as the person who was one day to correct the distorted image and to explain her. By now she trusted me to tell a different and more truthful story. I made her a promise then and I am keeping it now.

At the time, as the afternoon had developed into an evening of chatter and giggles, it did not seem like a demand, far less an obligation. But since Diana's death my thoughts have turned back to that conversation. In life she was frequently misunderstood and misquoted, but at least then she was able to employ her own ways of setting records straight. Now only those who truly knew and loved her can do so.

She was undoubtedly a strong young woman, but even the strong feel pain, and a compulsion to rail against injustice. That Diana was also unusually sensitive made her swan-gliding, lofty, apparent indifference to criticism especially difficult for her to maintain. To me this explains her ability to release her pains in both laughter and tears when we were together—for she could trust very few people when she needed to express her true self. She had, perforce, become an expert dissembler, fibber and manipulator. She had many masks, and I think it was a relief for her when she could sometimes drop them.

By then we were friends but even so, or possibly because of this, I sometimes had to be forthright with

Diana, and while this could be the cause of brief friction between us, it was this very trait which made her confident that I would tell the truth about her and not be intimidated by anyone who tried to stop me. She knew that in her I usually saw a cheerful young woman who loved life and men and good food and fun—someone very far from the pathetic, neurotic and lonely creature that she was often represented as being. She knew, too, that people underestimated her intelligence and wildly overestimated her self-obsessions—indeed, she had reached the point at which she found it relatively flattering when she was described in the press as being a 'loose cannon' within the royal family and the Establishment. Diana might not yet have fully matured into the woman she believed she was destined to be, but she wanted the world to know about her recovery and that it was a triumphant expression of independence and purpose. She wanted me to set that record straight.

Sometimes I'd find her, irritated and stretched on one of the sofas in the little sitting room, a tabloid newspaper strewn around her feet. Even the fact that some tiny detail in a story about her public or private life was wrong would enrage or frustrate her because, in her position, she knew she should appear to be above such concerns and yet she needed to straighten things out somehow. Even if the bald facts of a story were correct she still yearned to be able to offer her interpretation of things. But how could this be squared with her need for privacy? Certain privileged journalists would be pleased to take her call and write a story to correct things, or even to offer misleading information, but Diana knew that doing this too often would alienate writers on other, rival, newspapers. Since these might then fan the negative

rumours which centred upon her alleged wish to ma-
nipulate people, her supposed self-pity and her aggressive use of the telephone, she was in a near-impossible
situation. Desperate to put across her side of things and
to have her version of the truth known, she was still miserably aware that if she attempted to intervene yet further gossipy spins could be put on whatever she said.

All I could do was listen. And advise as any friend
would. I was well aware that my own background enabled me to be no more, or less, than a friend to Diana.
Whatever the reasons for our first meeting, these had become irrelevant history by the time she aired her frustrations to me at Kensington Palace. It wasn't quite like
Strangers on a Train because by then we knew each other
quite well, but I was aware that it was sometimes easier
for Diana to explain things to me, simply because our
other lives were so different.

1

Strange Meeting

I had watched the wedding of the Prince of Wales and Lady Diana Spencer through a haze of anaesthetic and pain, recovering from minor surgery in a London clinic. Seeing her that day, I felt that we were connected in a very powerful way, and that at some time in the future this connection would be proved. There was nothing logical about this premonition, and later I put it down to my drug-altered state of mind. Truthfully, I had taken no more interest in Diana before the marriage than had the average person enchanted by the heady idea of it all. To this day I still don't understand why I felt such certainty, but some insights defy analysis. Years later, however, when Diana and I knew each other very well, we were to agree that in some past life we might have been cousins, sisters, perhaps even mother and daughter. It seemed to be the only way to explain the depth of the rapport between us.

But like most people on that peerless July day in 1981 I merely thought that the marriage of Prince Charles to Lady Diana was a glorious piece of royal theatre. I wished them both well, shared in something of the world's romantic optimism about them, and returned to dealing with my own life.

Sixteen years later, in the early hours of 31 August 1997, I was in bed at home when I sleepily took a call from a friend who gave me the news of the car accident in Paris, after which I turned on the television. Astonishingly, I can't remember who rang, although I do remember my young nephew calling soon afterwards to ask if I needed him to come over. And I recall trying to reach the journalist Richard Kay, a true friend to the Princess, and to me.

I have very little recollection of the days after her death. I went into suspended animation, my emotions frozen. Although this might seem to be in chilly contrast to the massive nationwide—indeed, worldwide—flood of grief for Diana, it was nevertheless an expression of the same terrible sense of shock. Most of the millions who laid flowers down or signed condolence books were marking a genuine and deeply felt sadness for the waste of a woman who, although they had never met her, had somehow managed to touch human nerves and chords with her extraordinary magic and inherent goodness. It was not quite the same for me, however.

I'm not saying that Diana's death affected those of us who really knew her in a more *important* way, but that the grief, being personal, was *differently* powerful. Now, as I look back on my friendship with her, I see a thousand shimmering glimpses of the complex, caring, sometimes capricious, but always human princess. I feel privileged to have those memories. When someone you really care for dies there is often a frustrating sense of unfinished business. There is not a single day when I do not want to complete old, interrupted conversations, or share a funny anecdote with her, or simply give her a hug. I have to remind myself that love is not buried with the coffin any more than friendship is always begun with a formal handshake.

Ours had begun, it seems, with my premonition on her wedding day, although neither of us knew of it at the time. Only a month later, something else was to have a much more immediately profound effect on me. Yet this family crisis was to draw me inexorably and, perhaps inevitably, towards Diana.

When, in a hospital in August 1981, I saw a rainbow aura emanating from the motionless body of my nineteen-year-old sister Rachel, who had been severely injured in a road accident days before, I found that I could communicate with her, despite the coma that she would remain in for many months. I began to wonder if I had some real healing gift beyond vague instincts which I'd been aware of for some time. Over countless visits I saw how if I placed my hands near—not *on*—Rachel and concentrated whilst quietly speaking loving, encouraging words, the needle on the machine monitoring her heart would flicker and then jump. Intuitively, I somehow saw that her aura and spirit were floating above her physical body, and in some way I knew that I could help Rachel to pull the two forces together. Much later, I learned that hearing is the strongest of the senses, and that it continues to work however comatose a person might seem to be. Without considering my gift very much at the time, and certainly without quite yet believing that I could truly be a healer, my bond with my desperately ill sister nevertheless shaped me.

Indeed, to a significant extent I owe the rest of *my* life to Rachel, for through her survival I was made to confront the reality of my abilities: no longer could I imagine that they were accidents, coincidences or just some slight talent that could not be developed. Don't mistake me— the credit for Rachel's recovery is due to the care she received, but I do know that when the hospital had all but given up on her I had absolute belief that through love a great part of her could be saved. There is much truth in the old cliché about life being sustained by hope.

Years later, I found out that Rachel had met Diana— long before I did—when the young Princess of Wales visited the small unit in the Northamptonshire hospital where a crucial stage of Rachel's long recovery was accomplished. Some of Rachel's very first, newly relearned words might well have been to Diana.

Little in my background could have steered me towards, far less prepared me for, anything so unconventional as working as a professional healer. We lived in a large house in a North London suburb and my father, Harold, was a successful clothing manufacturer with a factory in the East End. He had happy memories of playing with Ronnie Scott and his band at jazz clubs before he acquired all his domestic and professional responsibilities, and was capable at times of reverting to an earlier wildness and unconventionality. My mother, Frances, was beautiful and, like Dad, artistic and poetic, so I suppose I inherited a little talent and some reckless instincts from both of them. But we were far from bohemian as a family. For my two younger sisters and me, life was fairly ordered, and my teenaged rebellions were stifled rather than encouraged.

Lots of teenaged girls avidly read their horoscopes but this all seemed far too tame for me. My best friend at school, Julia, was interested in palmistry and I fancied myself as something of a seer, so when we were about fourteen we formed an occult group and placed an advertisement in the *Jewish Chronicle* for members. My parents maintained an amused, detached tolerance about this: certainly I was never mocked or admonished. Meetings were held at Julia's parents' house near by. It was all perfectly innocent and harmless, and rooted mainly in a fascination with what the future might hold. At some level, however, I must have been seriously driven, because when I was seventeen I joined the Spiritualist Association of Great Britain.

But then I left school and had to get a job. Firstly, and very briefly, I worked in one of those couture dress shops where sales assistants flattered 'Madam' into expensive and unwise purchases because their commission depended upon it. After two or three days of informing potential customers that their favoured outfits didn't suit them at all, I was sacked. I then thought I'd try being a secretary, reasoning that, as I could play the piano, typewriter keys would be a doddle. I was proved right, and enjoyed my year working for a children's charity for £10 a week, even though it took me a little while to get the hang of carriage return and carbon copies.

Other office jobs followed and then there was a spell at my father's Old Street factory where we made clothes for big, big women. Even so, I learned a lot about the fashion business and despite the fact that, ironically, as the boss's daughter I was granted no favours and had to work like a skivvy, I really enjoyed it. Indeed, I think I could have made a career in that world. But then, just as I had landed a job with the distinguished designer Polly Peck as a fashion sketcher—something which would have combined my new skills with my frustrated artistic abilities—I tore the tendons in my hand and had to have surgery followed by three months' physiotherapy. By the time I was able to draw again the job had gone to someone else.

Circumstance had taken me to a place of healing, and after my recovery I began to work where I had been mended, as a secretarial temp at the Royal Free Hospital in Hampstead. At first I simply filed X-ray cards, then I learned something about radiography, and eventually I became a fully fledged medical secretary for a specialist in endocrinology. I now began to feel like a frustrated doctor, particularly as I had by then read widely about the influence of our glands, the whole complicated glandular system which affects our physical and emotional health so much. But I didn't seriously consider plunging into a formal medical training because by then, thanks to a wonderful and influential friend and my experience with Rachel, I was much more attuned to alternative methods of healing. Seven or eight years had passed and although Rachel had short-term memory problems, and always will have, I had seen how much better she was. I was certain that my silent willing for her recovery helped, and I tentatively trusted my powers enough to offer informal advice to friends.

Accident-prone as ever, I fractured my coccyx in 1990, having slipped on some spilled milk in a supermarket. Hardly the most profoundly mystic of conversions, but that's what it turned out to be. After several years of pain and mind-numbing paperwork, legal aid and persistence, I was awarded some money in compensation. In the meantime, however, I had been forced to give up full-time work. As it happened, though, knowledge of my abilities as a healer had spread by word of mouth, and I was able to scrape a living by seeing people at home. By now I was particularly interested in working with clients' auras, the extraordinary waves of colour that can be seen to surround a human body, colours which will alter with mood and with the state of an individual's health. These auras are no less than a map of the psyche and the well-being, or otherwise, of each of us. (For an explanation of some of my methods, and of Diana's interest in becoming a healer, see Appendix.)

Only a few decades ago many people found it hard to accept the idea that physical and emotional chemistry can influence human behaviour. Today, however, most people understand that although such matters can't always be logically explained, their intuitions and impulses are often correct, however mysterious they may seem. I do appear to have an acute understanding of individuals' auras, and as a result I can see how and why some of the situations into which they have got themselves may be harmful or, conversely, for the best. This understanding is the basis from which some of my work stems. And my pre-eminent skill seems to be dealing with stress and offering healing in those circumstances.

From 1990, therefore, after my accident, I was working as a part-time healer. Of course I endured criticism and dismissive remarks from some members of the conventional medical establishment and occasionally this hurt—but I had faith in my work, and my results, so I continued. Nor did I always charge if I felt that my client would be further stressed and counter-productively strained by worrying about a bill.

My association with Diana began in 1993, the chance result of her well-known interest in alternative medicine. I have rarely met anyone so greatly in need of physical and emotional repair.

Her trust in me was rooted in the very fact that she was reassured that I was not on the same social circuit as other friends. There was no danger of me blurting out things to people to whom she might have been sending out different messages from her complicated private agenda. I was to learn that Diana was a great compartmentalizer, and she carved out a very precise box for me in her life. Few other people ever entered it. This didn't offend me, in fact it suited me well: I had no wish to be part of her society life. I just hoped that our friendship would enable her to cope with the darker facets of her life with greater confidence and assurance.

I don't think that she had a loving, accepting and understanding circle of friends when she was a little girl, or even as a young woman. Later, when she was Princess of Wales and so many people were making demands upon her, or courting her attention, or flattering her, she had even fewer opportunities to make real friends. That is why, I believe, she responded to me, and why we gradually came first to trust each other, and then to become friends. The fact that I was several years older than she, and came from a suburban Jewish background which could scarcely have contrasted more with her privileged, patrician one, made no difference. True communication recognizes no formal boundaries or obstacles.

As with some of my clients, I knew that I could send healing energies to Diana through touch and presence, and even simply down the telephone. Nor did I take a judgemental line with her as a conventional psychotherapist might have done. The very fact that Diana trusted me, a friend and informal adviser, more than some of the specialists towards whom her family, and her husband's, tried to lead her suggests that, in talking over her problems with me, she was expressing a little rebellion of her own. I don't think she ever quite forgave some of Prince Charles's relations or influential friends for suggesting, when she and Charles were still together, albeit very unhappily so, that she be consigned to some residential clinic for treatment. (Diana mentioned to me that they had wanted her to go to 'a nut house' or a 'loony bin' but that she had refused to go. She always seemed completely compos mentis to me.) My methods are considerably more gentle.

About that first meeting late in 1993. I remember the Princess's formal suit, her huge Chanel handbag, her wide smile and her insistence that I address her as 'Diana'. I also remember feeling that about three great truckloads of negative emotional waste were extracted that afternoon while we talked and I analysed her aura.

Some time later I was shocked to see on her traces of the scratches and scabs of recent self-mutilation. I thought I detected rakings from the evenly spaced tines of a fork in the patterns of scraping, but whatever the instrument used, all the marks would have been concealed by everyday clothes.

The public had been led to suppose that Diana's tendency to attack herself had ceased years ago. In this the public had been misled, however. A deep build-up of residual pain resulting from the end of her doomed affair with Captain James Hewitt in the early 1990s, coupled with a desperately unsuccessful attempt to form a relationship with someone else shortly afterwards, had left Diana as damaged as ever. She had recently been trying to wound herself in a misguided attempt to win the love and sympathy of a man she felt was neglecting and rejecting her.

Already emotionally weakened by the death of her father, Earl Spencer, in 1992, Diana bore the physical and emotional scars of a fragile heart broken twice in recent succession, as well as her greatest pain—the anguish brought on by the death throes of a marriage which, even as late as 1994, she still hoped could be saved.

Obviously, at our first meeting, I could only observe the Princess and silently draw some conclusions which were themselves worrying enough, even though she wasn't then marked by self-laceration. When I saw the scabs and scratches soon afterwards I still felt that I did not yet know her well enough to pass any comment; indeed, it was to be some time before I could be quite open with her. Even the surprising informality of our early meetings was unnerving. Diana enabled me to overcome most of my shyness almost at once, although despite her friendly manner I could sense, as well as see, how troubled she was.

From the start I could feel the depth and force of her tensions. I suppose I must have released some of them because at one point she smiled and said I had 'otherworldly' eyes. I could only mumble back something about how extraordinary her own eyes were. I was there to make a start—things were unlikely, I reminded myself, to be mended, let alone perfected, all at once. And yet what began as a consultation shifted over the next few years as Diana and I became close.

The remarkable thing about Diana, even during that first meeting, was that she was so receptive to ideas that other people might have dismissed. Some time later, presumably having felt that some emotional toxins had been drawn away from her body, she asked me if I could do the same for buildings, and suggested that I might clear some of the 'ghosts' of Kensington Palace one day. I wasn't ready for that yet, and neither, actually, was she. Thus, my first visit to the palace that was her home only took place after we had established the beginnings of a deep trust. She laughed in disbelief, however, when I asked for her address as we made this arrangement, and said I must have been the only person in the world who didn't know where she lived.

When my father died in 1996, for months I was too upset to work much at all. One of the people who helped me in my grief was Diana. She herself had a raw and recent memory of the death of a beloved father, in the same year in which she and Prince Charles had separated. Nor did the fact that her relationship with her father had often been stormy stem the force of her grief. Often, in fact, things are worse for the child when a parent dies before old wounds and misunderstandings have been resolved and laid to rest, buried at the funeral alongside the coffin. In 1996, however, the tables were turned, for then it was Diana who supported *me*, hugged me as we wept together. No matter where she was, there was no time, night or day, at which she would not be willing to talk to me on the telephone and help if she could. She had a healer's instincts—I know this now.

There were times when I had to ask Diana 'Who's the healer here?' because I would talk to her about troubles in my own life that I seldom discussed with anyone else. She could be very supportive and took a real interest in my fears and worries, as she did in my family. I had, for instance, something of a weight problem when I first met her. I had put on weight when a serious relationship collapsed two years before I met Diana, and I was having trouble in shedding it. I could talk to her about this, and found her constructively sympathetic, observing that so great had been the emotional pain generated by the collapse of my relationship that I was holding on to my weight both in self-protection and in physical proof that my relationship had once been solid and demonstrably real. She described my weight as armour, simultaneously protecting me from further injury and repelling men so that the chance of another potentially hurtful relationship became remote. By coincidence, perhaps, I was soon able to take control of this physical problem of mine and little by little have lost much of the excess weight.

By then our relationship had altered slightly, for we had become friends and she had learned to trust me when she needed advice. I offered everything I could with all my heart, and I can never forget that it was Diana—in all her patience and generosity—who helped me to pick up my own crazy fragments, to live again and work again. For this gift of support and strength alone I will always remember her with the deepest affection, gratitude and respect.

Diana wasn't perfect. Like all humans she was paradoxical, capricious, difficult at times, troubled, mercurial and inconsistent, as well as loyal, brave and affectionate. Recognition and acceptance of her complexities does not diminish her. I take it as a compliment that she exposed all her sides to me—as her true friend.

2

Kensington Palace Days

Apart from my parents, very few people knew that Diana and I had become friends. This wasn't just because she wanted to keep our friendship a secret, but also because I didn't want to be placed in the position of having to deflect questions when fascinated friends from other areas of my life evinced the inevitable curiosity. Moreover, our relationship became a two-way thing and *I* needed privacy too.

Close and intimate conversations between us began soon after Diana invited me to visit Kensington Palace and cleanse or exorcise it of residual bad energy from her marriage. Expecting to get lost, I was driven there by a friend that first time. Later I would often take a cab, and remember one particular taxi driver who had come to Britain from the former Soviet Union by way of Israel. He was almost in tears when he dropped me at Kensington Palace, touchingly honoured to be in the Princess of Wales's driveway.

I was admitted by Diana's butler, Paul Burrell, who had begun his life at Kensington Palace as a footman seconded from Buckingham Palace and who, famously, had been at the top of Diana's wish list when she was asked what she wanted to take with her when the marital

household was divided. Paul was a trusted ally to us both
on many occasions.

At the time, Kensington Palace had only relatively recently become home to Diana alone. The nineteen rooms
that made up the apartments still bore the stamp and carried the weight of the years when she had lived there with
Charles, and it was this residual atmosphere that Diana
wanted me to help her change. It was not that she did not
respect the beauty and importance of many of the pictures and antique pieces that remained there, but she
needed the lingering effects of Charles's influence to be
dispelled. We had some tea and then she began to show
me around. My first impressions were mixed: I could
understand Diana's wishes, but as someone who has always been affected by outstanding paintings, I could not
help but gaze in admiration at many of them.

In the end we agreed that there were too many rooms
for me to cleanse properly all at once—it is an immensely
exhausting process for healers because they must use
their force to counter negative energy in the rooms and
perhaps absorb some of it. Anyway, it was probably appropriate if some of the more formal rooms in Diana's
suite retained something of the grandeur of her status as
Princess of Wales. The majority of Charles's most cherished personal things were to be moved to his new home
at St James's Palace and other items were discreetly as-
signed to some royal basement, perhaps to be stacked
alongside boxes and crates of gifts sent to Charles and
Diana, acknowledged but never used, during the years of
their marriage. I stood in doorways, willing hostile or
unhappy spirits to depart. There were even traces of
these energies in parts of Diana's private suite. In a way I
was pleased that time was short—she had an evening en-

gagement to prepare for—because this intense 'ghost-hopping', as she called it, had worn me out.

I had been heartened to see that her inner sanctum, her relatively small and most personal rooms, had already been lifted with bright, pale paints and fabrics. Modern pictures were hung alongside cheerful artwork sent by children or dedicated to 'Mummy' by William and Harry. In her private sitting room there was a large sofa facing the TV, a sophisticated CD and stereo system and, in front of the hearth, the huge stuffed hippopotamus on which her children would lounge. I usually preferred to sit on the floor and often came to prop myself up against that hippo. The room was tidy but comfortable, humanized by a little clutter. The lighting was subtle and soft. In the heart of a palace Diana had made a real home for herself, her sons and their friends.

Upstairs at Kensington Palace there was a well-equipped little kitchen, very clinical and stainless-steely, where the boys' meals would sometimes be prepared. Diana scarcely used it, however, preferring to use the huge, staffed one. She was so proud when she eventually learned how to heat a ready-made pasta meal or 'cook' a baked potato in the microwave oven. Then, having torn the cellophane wrapping off a store's pre-prepared salad, she might proudly present an informal supper. At other times she might prepare her speciality, the superb bacon sandwich she had learned to fix for herself and friends when she lived in a flat in South Kensington before her marriage. Sometimes she'd guiltily warm through a croissant for her breakfast as if expecting to be scolded for such a minor indulgence. I enjoyed all such offerings and never chided her about not learning to cook 'properly' (even though she had attended a cordon bleu course in

Wimbledon after she left school), and it became something of a standing joke between us. Where was the incentive when there was a restaurant-standard kitchen at her disposal, with staff in attendance, if 'the Boss'—as her employees always called Diana—wanted anything more complex than a snack? The staff were, of course, always on hand if she was entertaining on any scale.

One night, well over two years after I'd 'cleansed' the place, Diana called me at home in panic about a bad, lingering smell. Could there be some dangerous, lurking spirit, one that I had failed to clear? I asked her where it seemed to be coming from and she said she thought it could be her kitchen, so I suggested she retrace all her most recent steps. After she had been all over the apartments, it transpired that, having prepared a simple supper for friends and then done the washing-up, she had blown out the pilot lights of her grill and cooker, believing, as she put it, that 'Some idiot had left them on.' That explained the smell. I suggested that she call British Gas, but she was more than canny enough to realize that if she did that the incident might be on all the front pages the following morning. My idea that she should inform the palace security guards was also rejected on the grounds that the news would soon spread via the Kensington Palace bush telegraph. So I said that she should open all the kitchen windows, close the door and leave a large note for Paul Burrell wherever he might first see it when he arrived the next morning. She did so—taking ages, because the old sash windows were difficult to free—and called me back, giggling, before going to bed. All was made well when the dependable Paul (she always called him 'Perky Paul') dealt discreetly with the situation the following morning.

It wasn't hard to imagine how heady the small freedoms Diana was enjoying by 1994, in and out of the kitchen, contrasted with the Kensington Palace routines of the early days of her marriage. The very young girl who had briefly enjoyed some independence with her flatmates had eaten out with friends most evenings or fixed herself a convenience snack like the rest of us. She hadn't had to learn many of the skills of household management. When she was expected, soon afterwards, to approve a week's worth of menus in advance, Diana was probably as baffled and fearful as was the new Mrs de Winter, the heroine of Daphne du Maurier's *Rebecca*, under the cold and unflickering gaze of the housekeeper, Mrs Danvers.

Perhaps in defiant response to the often chilly formality of the days before her separation from Prince Charles, Diana's bedroom was a relaxed and almost 'girlie' place, filled with cushions, frills, white lace and photographs in frames, a style almost certainly too cluttered for Charles's masculine, spartan tastes. There were spears and stumps of her favourite scented candles as well, along with fluffy toys arranged upon the chaise below her bed, seeming almost to guard the room and protect its occupant. Feminine and predominantly pastel, it was the kind of room certainly easier to maintain for those who have maids visiting every day and if the laundry is seen to several times a week.

Her everyday clothes were mainly kept in a large room close to her bedroom, stored carefully by colour and season. The ballgowns and other formal designer outfits were stored in a lower room, but here in Diana's 'wardrobe' she could fling open the door and choose the leggings, sweatshirt, jersey or informal T-shirt she wanted to wear that day.

The Boss could, however, be very fussy about how even her most casual clothes were ordered. She once dismissed a dresser because she found that socks and underwear had just been hurled carelessly into drawers once too often. She was not unique in this behaviour, however. It may have been after that occasion that Diana—always keen to pick up on the Kensington Palace grapevine—learned, during one of her herbal-tea-drinking sessions with the staff in her big kitchen that a dresser for another member of the royal family had lost her job. The woman had recently found out that she had breast cancer and in her miserable and exhausted state had explained her situation to her employer. She was dismissed. Appalled, Diana tried to rehire the Portuguese woman on a part-time basis but was prevented by Kensington Palace protocol. Angered and frustrated, she at least made sure that the dresser was informed about her legal rights in this sad situation.

It should be remembered that Kensington Palace is a vast place, containing many separate households, from those of Princess Margaret, the Kents and Gloucesters, several ancient duchesses and aunts, to many smaller grace-and-favour apartments, some of which are occupied by servants of the Crown, including Sir Robert and Lady Jane Fellowes, Diana's elder sister. No wonder Prince Charles humorously echoed his great-uncle Edward VIII's remark and referred to the place as 'the Aunt Heap'. And no wonder, too, that a mischievous Diana rather relished the 'downstairs' gossip she picked up when she ventured to her kitchens to share a break with her staff.

This apparent informality of hers could be deceptive, however. The therapies which Diana remained almost addicted to in 1994 and 1995 could create a relaxed impression, but she was still on a very short fuse. She wanted the approval of simple and decent people whom she respected, but she also craved privacy and the deference which her position brought. If she felt that protocol had been breached and that a little too much informality was evident 'below stairs', the culprit could be chilled by a glare from those laser-blue eyes and then ignored completely until Diana had forgotten the small offence— whatever it might have been. Naturally this created its own tensions.

Having said this, and even though anyone who worked for the Princess at Kensington Palace was obliged to sign a pledge of confidentiality, I find it interesting that after all those years, and especially in the year since Diana's death, not one of her staff has stepped forward to say that he or she was treated unfairly. Staff wages improved after Diana's divorce, and if any true injustice had taken place human nature and gossip would have taken their course and the world would now have stark 'facts' about the harpy of KP. Instead, there have only been the small bruised rounds of gossipy grudge and upset common to any establishment with a few disaffected members of staff.

When we first met in 1993 Diana was a pathetically damaged creature, no longer capable of even aspiring to emulate the swan which glides along the water with regal ease; the swan had tired of straining furiously beneath the smooth surface. In public the cracks were beginning to show. Her marriage had proved to be a miserable sham. A trusted and adored lover, James Hewitt, had publicly betrayed her, and then she fell for a married man who was in no position to return her love; as a result she dropped into another pit of rejection. Added to this, the father whose love she had sought all her life had died, while her sister Jane had, by her marriage to Sir Robert Fellowes, the Queen's private secretary, close associations with the royal family; thus it was understandable that Diana had come to see even Jane as being in the enemy camp.

She felt abandoned, rejected and broken. Depression can be the most debilitating of illnesses; while it was a good thing that she recognized that she needed help, at that time she was unable to understand that some of her many different therapies were counteracting each other, possibly harmfully. That Diana was addicted to exercise is well known—she relished the temporary endorphin rush and feel-good effects of running and other strenuous exercises. Obviously she also liked how it toned her figure and heightened her good looks. But I saw her as a therapy junkie as well, turning trustingly towards any new branch of healing which she felt offered her hope. Any friend who raved about this treatment or that would be grilled for details and contact numbers—and few in the profession seemed unwilling to offer help. Equally, few offered her the best and bitterest medicine of all— the truth.

Osteopathy, reflexology, acupuncture, shiatsu, massage, colonic irrigation, aromatherapy—these were just some of the treatments Diana turned to, as well as seeking the advice of a famous expert in eating disorders. To make matters worse she was misreading the already confused and conflicting advice she was offered from every quarter. Even though she had sometimes paid handsomely for treatments designed to make her relax, I soon realized that Diana's bright but rather manic conversational manner was an expression of tension and panic. When I first knew her she was afraid of silences and mistook peaceful calm for the evidence of an awkward barrier. Her genuine emotional destitution was palpable—between us we had to strip away not merely emotional clutter but some of the ideas she'd absorbed from healers, in order to identify her most pressing needs and then decide how they should be met.

One of Diana's very deepest needs was for companionship—in short, she was lonely. Sometimes her perceived hunger for therapists and healers was underpinned by simple, lonely boredom and a desperate need to be nurtured and understood.

Because Diana's therapies were her props, it took time to wean her away from some of them, and certainly she at first resisted many of my attempts to help her. I was unlike most of the people who surrounded her in other compartments of her life, flattering, pampering or agreeing with everything she said. If I felt she was wasting her time or money, if I believed that she was mistaken in thinking that she needed to cover all therapeutic options, or if she was enduring unnecessary treatments elsewhere, I would tell her so. Once she had come to know that my views were not driven by self-interest or financial considerations she listened more carefully. So far as I could see, by 1995 she was in pretty good physical shape except for her weak back, and I therefore felt that she should now concentrate on this and upon the spiritual aspects of healing.

But our friendship wasn't all lecturing and finger-wagging. Far from it; indeed, we'd often be giggling too much to work very hard. Once, Diana took off her shoes and tights and showed me that her legs were marked like a zebra's. *What on earth?!* I could barely speak. Ruefully, but with a huge smile, she told me that she'd been to see a healer who had taped bands of pulverized rocks across her legs. She had been sunbathing recently, and since the top layer of skin had also been removed when she ripped off the 'bandages' she was left with the zebra stripes. Fortunately the effect didn't last long.

At first Diana found my bluntness rather startling. In fact, this is the way I am with everyone, and in her case I felt that creepy-crawling from other quarters had been extremely damaging. She didn't describe it as such, but by her accounts of this continuous flattery I guessed it must be so. I've seen lots of therapy junkies over the years and simply wanted to steer her towards her strengths rather than allowing her to dwell upon imagined weaknesses. It was not an easy task. In 1993 and 1994 Diana still had such low self-esteem that she thought she needed other people's deference to prove that she was worthy of attention and affection. Far from signifying vanity, her apparent preoccupation with her looks was another expression of her insecurity. Inside she still felt like the rather mousy, tall and gawky girl who, she believed, had failed to please her father and who had been powerless when her mother Frances had abandoned the family; indeed, nothing could ever quite shake Diana's belief that she had somehow caused her parents' divorce. Now, worst of all, the loveliest clothes, a near-perfect figure and the best blond highlights in the world had failed to bind Prince Charles to her.

She felt she hadn't pleased her husband enough when she became pregnant, and may then have remembered that her adored brother, Charles Spencer, seemed only to be attracted to the most willowy of women. She became thin, but that didn't do the trick. Prince Charles's attachment to Camilla Parker Bowles remained undiminished and after Diana gave birth again her husband merely evinced a cautious pleasure in the arrival of another son. Even then, he complained at Harry's christening that the little prince was blighted with the sandy Spencer colouring. Mindful again that Charles Spencer had married the beautiful but wraithlike former model Victoria Lockwood, towards whom Diana developed a sisterly affection, she became thin again—even thinner. Yet nothing could please her husband as much as the company of another, older, woman. When her two subsequent romantic involvements left Diana rejected and stranded, her self-esteem—never very high to begin with—dropped to less than zero and she became almost wholly dependent on the bolstering, if often fickle or false, affections of sycophants and public opinion. What she needed when I first knew her were self-acceptance and self-reliance.

As time passed and our friendship consolidated, Diana came to confide in me about her past, and found that I was always willing to listen and offer reassurance if necessary. Years earlier, as the fiancée of the Prince of Wales, the then Lady Diana Spencer had declared that she was as thick as a plank. This statement proclaimed a kind of desperate false modesty that actually begged for someone to answer that she was wrong, that she was in fact highly intelligent. Similarly, there was a kind of double bluff about her beauty. The truth is that she never really believed in it, and was too insecure to face the world without her armour of glamour. Although she displayed it often enough in bikinis and ballgowns, Diana didn't even believe that she had a good body, and actually felt uncomfortable in the tight and fitted clothes that her public engagements often demanded. Countless times I saw her rush to her room upon returning from some official duty, flinging her hat down and kicking off her high heels as she went, to emerge minutes later dressed very differently. She was much happier (like most women, perhaps) in comfortable, loose clothing. Often we'd pore together over photographs taken at some function and she'd laugh scornfully at the 'awful' outfit or hat duty had constrained her to wear.

I wanted to help Diana rebuild—or maybe even discover—her sense of self-esteem. In a funny way I was repaying a debt.

Those many times later when I saw her at home at Kensington Palace, relaxed and barefoot, clad in old jeans and a loose T-shirt, I could observe a different face of beauty. By then I believe I had helped her to begin to find a confidence she had not realized she possessed, and although she was energized, she wasn't as alarmingly manic as she could be when I first met her. By then she could usually sleep without pills, she'd stopped crying about the wreck of her marriage and her fears for her boys had lessened. When she did shed tears, it was now without shame. Very importantly, by the time I was a regular at the palace in the mid-1990s, I was no longer glimpsing scratches on her chest or limbs.

As regards her physical fitness, Diana ran round Kensington Gardens every morning—sometimes at night, too, against my advice—and already ate very sensibly on the whole, despite mistaken assumptions to the contrary among people at large. She believed notions about her poor nutrition to have been fanned by hostile courtiers loyal to other members of the royal family. Although she rarely ate a traditionally healthy breakfast and loved huge cups of strong coffee in the morning, she also drank a lot of fruit and vegetable juices. She was largely vegetarian and loved light pasta dishes, but depending on her mood she could happily munch chocolate or declare a longing for her bacon sandwich or some grilled fish or chicken breast for lunch. She was physically a young, fit and strong woman, one who could follow her appetite's instincts. But she could be inconsistent and paradoxical about this. I think I was the first person to reassure her that it was OK for her to backslide occasionally and that she didn't have to be apologetic about it or to descend to coy 'naughty-little-girl' mode, as though pleading for forgiveness. I knew it was a cliché, but Diana's eyes glinted when I told her that 'a little of what you fancy does you good.'

Something much more elusive than muscular aches, something spiritual and emotional, had needed to be fixed. When she was largely mended inside and her depression had lifted, the pains in Diana's back, neck and stomach retreated markedly. They never quite disappeared and her back was always to be her weakest place, despite the fact that she had dancer's limbs that were unusually flexible and strong. These pains had not been purely psychosomatic—over-manipulation in some areas had seriously damaged bone and cartilage. In any case, I reject the opinions of those who dismiss psychosomatic or referred pain as being unworthy of concern: pain is pain, even if it is 'felt' in an amputated limb.

Even after she had been largely healed, however, Diana's body was able to release copious amounts of bile. It is no accident that the dictionary includes 'bile' as a synonym for anger. Only months before she died, when she was in great physical shape, she remained impelled to have her colonic treatment as often as once a week. Some years ago, when colonic irrigation first caught the public imagination, one *Vogue* or *Harper's & Queen* writer who had undergone the treatment wrote amusingly of wishing farewell to the remains of some sandwich she'd had for lunch years earlier. Residual sludge from Diana's colon would long since have been removed, but she continued with her frequent treatments because they left her energized and headily released of emotional blockages. She once said to me with endearing frankness when she was about to set off for a colonic, 'I'm going to have my bum washed out.' I found it astonishing that this young woman—who barely drank alcohol, who exercised and who ate so sensibly—still had so much bile to discharge through her intestines, even as late as 1997. There must have been so much stress and unresolved anger, too. But her stresses were greater and more deeply internalized than those of the average person and most of the time she felt obliged to present an image of perfection whilst coping with them.

Through memory of her own pain and suffering Diana was able genuinely to empathize with the trials and wounds of others. There was nothing artificial about these concerns, and those who have suggested that she had set out to sanctify herself are mistaken. No one forced her to work as hard as she did for her charities, and much of this work was accomplished privately. Other members of the royal family have been pleased to be associated with charities and other worthy enterprises— one of Princess Margaret's favourites is said to be the Migraine Trust, for instance—but they seldom do more than offer patronage and allow their name to head the writing paper. With the exceptions, perhaps, of those of the dedicated Princess Royal and the Duchess of Kent, royal 'good works' can seem to be more concerned with gala dinners and glad-handing than the committed, quiet work at the coalface of often unfashionable causes which Diana preferred.

Diana had a low boredom threshold and, while highly intelligent, she did not have much of what is called an inner life. Constant distractions are often necessary for those who cannot be at peace alone and who have trouble distinguishing between silence and rejection, solitude and loneliness. If there was a task at hand—if she had to bone up for a speech or steep herself in complicated background information relating to an engagement— no one could have been more dedicated than Diana. I saw her concentration as she studied *Gray's Anatomy* in order to learn as much about the complex functions of the human heart as any medical student before she went to witness an operation at the Brompton Hospital. But alone and without other purpose she would more often flick on the TV. She might easily do some back-stretching exercises on the carpet as she watched, relishing this small pocket of freedom and privacy at the end of the day. Paul Burrell would probably have arranged for supper to be brought to her on a tray, but if he'd gone home she might fix herself a baked potato and an egg. At times she would be quite content, but occasionally she would be wistful. At other times she would listen to a favourite piece of classical music (she particularly liked the nineteenth-century Russian composers, and I'd given her many CDs of ballet music), call a friend or perhaps try to reach one of her sons before she would even consider reading a book for pleasure.

Diana responded to poetry or to philosophical writings if they were placed before her, and enjoyed romantic novels, but she was not someone who could often lose herself in classic literature or biography, or find peace and distraction in a dry study of art or ideas, however much the *practical* expression of those same ideas might have interested her. If she had no programme of engagements on any particular day she would cast around for diversion. Perhaps she couldn't reach the boys, the hairdresser had come and gone, there was nothing much on the TV, a favourite friend wasn't free to drop everything and meet her for lunch. And while there were certainly good healthy things in the larder at home, her fiercest hungers were seldom connected with food. Her craving for stimulation might be initially satisfied by something as simple or shallow as a change of clothes—but then she would want company.

A profound sense of dissatisfaction beyond idle boredom often led Diana's hand to stray towards the telephone; indeed, the phone may well have been her most significant addiction. She was, in short, something of a telephone junkie, spending at least £3,000 a month on her mobile-phone bill. During the time I was involved with her we would speak for hours a day—eight hours was not unusual, although the record was fourteen. She spent nearly every free minute of the day on the telephone. It was certainly a dependency, and it is one that I share, although as dependencies go it has to be a pretty harmless one—if one can afford it. Once, in 1994, Diana opened her handbag and showed me no fewer than four mobiles, each with the call-waiting facility so that she wouldn't miss a single person who had returned her call and might, if they had not hung up, be able to speak to them on one phone while she tried to make yet another call on a different line. To the end there were friends like me or Richard Kay whom she would call whenever she wanted a gossipy chat. But back in the early and mid-1990s, before she found a higher purpose, she would probably ring any healer, therapist or astrologer who was prepared to listen to her.

At that point in her life Diana's main source of self-worth and self-esteem came from her knowledge that, if nothing else, she was making a massive success of being a mother. Within a very few years she would come to realize that she could do, and be, even more than this, but for now she felt she had things to prove. I tried—and to some extent succeeded—in disabusing her of the notion that this was necessary. None the less she retained an obsession with 'paying back' for all her privileges. Self-doubt made her imagine that if she was guilty of back-sliding even once in some diet or exercise regime she would have rendered wasted all the previous effort and discipline. Similarly, she felt compelled to maintain her level of caring work, as though she didn't trust in her ability to pick up the pieces and resume things if she let herself down occasionally.

When I saw the pain she was still enduring about her failed marriage, the fiasco of her broken relationship with James Hewitt and the debris of a more recent friendship with Oliver Hoare, a married art dealer for whom she had developed an intense crush which proved to be tiresome for him and destructive for her, I thought that, as her friend, I should try to make her understand that she was no more to blame for these sadnesses than she had been for the breakdown of her parents' marriage. I tried to make her understand that endings are not always failures—that not all relationships are meant to be for life. The keys to her self-castigation as an adult all lay within the childhood baggage she lugged behind her, and in her dangerous tendency to repeat childish patterns of subsuming her own identity in doomed attempts to please others. Only when she found self-respect, I told her, would she be able to accept her mistakes, her human frailty and an appropriate share of responsibility if things had gone wrong. None of the extremes she skittered between—those of the pathetic victim, the abjectly culpable cause of misery, or the almost messianic controller— were appropriate. I tried to show her that masochistically assuming complete blame for any bad situation is a twisted form of arrogance: that same attitude inevitably leads to a person taking all the credit when things have gone well.

But I also tried to be gentle and reassuring with her as we talked through her memories of her childhood and her parents' divorce. As a third daughter she believed she had been a disappointment to her parents, something which was confirmed to her when Earl and Countess Spencer separated shortly after the birth of Charles—the longed-for heir to Althorp. Self-pity afflicts all of us at times and, truthfully, there was nothing very unusual, among such aristocratic families, in Diana and her sisters and brother being cared for by nannies until they were old enough to go to boarding school. Even so, the special needs and insecurities of this particular child do *not* seem to have been acknowledged. She remained haunted by the memory of hearing, at the age of only six, her mother's high heels crunching on the gravel outside their home on the December afternoon in 1967 when Frances went away. Diana waited on the back steps every day for months, hoping her mother would return.

She must have been baffled. She may have thought it was somehow her fault. In any case, young Diana took on the role of carer to her baby brother, attempting to dress him in her teddy bear's outfits. Abandoned by her mother, largely ignored by her father and, with her siblings, publicly fought over in court in a widely publicized custody battle soon afterwards, the idea of the importance of family stability, and particularly of brooding maternal protection, took hold. She would never abandon *her* children, and she was to endure long humiliations before accepting that her marriage was in tatters. Those who assume guilt usually require absolution, and sometimes seek it through being as pleasing as possible to everyone, thereby becoming social chameleons. Or they may take up the visible penance of good works. Most retain a simultaneous need to be cherished as well as forgiven. Her sons could not love her more and her public popularity was unrivalled. But for a very long time these proofs of her worth were, for Diana, never quite enough.

Sometimes she would cry when we talked about all this. Occasionally there would be that most tragic type of weeping—sobbing without tears. I knew that my candour and questions had hit horribly raw and tender spots. It was painful for both of us, but honesty was the only way forward. I made it clear to her that she could not 'buy' my friendship by only listening to what she wanted to hear, and that if she wanted to please me I demanded the stretch and strain of trust and truthful self-examination. Repeatedly I begged her to try to be herself so that she could confront, consider and accept herself as a unique and valuable person, flawed, perhaps, but no more so than the rest of us . . .

We were still talking about this and working our way through some of her demons two years after we first met. Memories of all those years of trying to mould herself into someone acceptable to Prince Charles and his family, and of all those earlier years when she had bent herself into a semblance of the daughter she thought she ought to be, could not be quickly or easily erased; I even wondered if those emotional contortions had contributed to Diana's enduring spinal weakness. But by 1995 there was a distinct improvement which showed in little things, and by the following year she had begun to please *herself* in small ways. For instance, she would no longer automatically wear even a little make-up when we met, but only use some if it pleased her to do so. She had also had to overcome the barrier between herself and her anger and had found a better way of expressing it than self-mutilation. Eventually she could express her rage verbally and make no apology if anger was appropriate.

Diana was self-protective—she had been forced to learn to be—but that is not the same thing as consciously using people. Even when speaking to certain journalists I think she would have regarded it as two-way traffic: she had her point of view to put across, and they got a headline. By the same token she could drop someone if she believed that she was being used, or if she felt threatened. She would certainly think nothing of telephoning me scores of times in one day, and would assume I'd always be ready for a chat. But I didn't feel used when Diana did this sort of thing—it was my choice to take those calls and if I was too busy to speak at a particular moment I would tell her so, knowing that she'd feel a bit let down.

But even if I couldn't always take her call, we still talked endlessly on the phone. I remember one occasion when the conversation went on for ten hours and ranged from the trivial to the incredibly serious-minded. Sometimes we'd both watch a TV soap at our respective homes, each with our phones clamped to our ears, although we only disturbed each other's concentration if there was some extraordinary turn of events in the Street, the Close or the Square. Then, as the credits came up along with the theme tune, we'd start to analyse that episode's highlights. With *Casualty*—absolutely Diana's favourite TV programme—it was a different matter, however. While one can always catch up with a soap, each episode of the hospital drama is self-contained and Diana was never, ever, to be interrupted when she was watching it.

When I was there with her Diana would sometimes speak of a rather regretful fantasy about the life she might have planned for herself. It was to have been as far removed from the life of a dazzling star on the international stage as was possible. This dream existence was, naturally, one of cheerful comfort, and involved, inevitably, marriage and children. But above all, those fantasies of Diana's centred around loving, reciprocally supportive bonds with a man who took her and cherished her for what she was, a man who would be there for her twenty-four hours a day. He would be trustworthy, expressive, tactile, and he would encourage her to grow into her true self without resenting her for not being someone he had idealized.

There was no need to press Diana for elaboration during these small, sad, occasionally almost mad, flights of fancy—it was perfectly clear what she was talking about. But at a certain moment in 1996 these daydreams changed, almost as though a switch had been flicked. They no longer seemed to be the products of a sense of guilt, regret and personal failure, but were pitched forward with hope and optimism for the future. Like all of us, Diana longed to be someone's number one. The irony is that she *was* the nation's, even the world's, favourite. But she had not been her husband's first choice. The moment she was ready to accept this she could, and did, look ahead.

Thus, despite the phenomenal emotional transformation in Diana that I observed during the mid-1990s, the growth of all her strengths and the firming of her confidence, she was still, in 1995, a lost girl who hadn't yet achieved the most simple of ambitions—that of being the sole and undisputed centre of some man's life. Sometimes, too, she needed reassurance about her place in the hearts of the people whose love she must have known she could depend upon. An insecure Diana would still want to know the word on the street after some engagement, photo call, or speech, and this often led her to call me.

'What did people really think about it?' she would ask. *'Did I do OK?'*

3

Diana at Home

For Diana, a typical 'free' day—that is, a day without formal engagements—at Kensington Palace would begin with strong coffee quite early (she regarded a lie-in until eight as a rare indulgence). If her boys were away— at school or with their father—she would go to the gym for a good workout, or have her run in the palace gardens, her pace so fast that few strollers in the public areas would recognize the tall figure who dashed past them. Then it was back for a shower and the daily appointment with her hairdresser, before two or three hours' dealing with correspondence in her office with her two secretaries. Diana read every letter carefully and drafted replies which she would later check and sign.

It is worth noting, as an aside, that her hairdresser came to the palace every weekday, and I sometimes used to think that it was a bit of a waste of money if Diana was simply going to stay at home and be by herself or with me later. Even though she usually had just a wash and blow-dry, each of those hairdos would have cost quite a lot at the Daniel Galvin salon—the sort of price that many women would budget to spend maybe only four times a year.

If she was to lunch with friends Diana would change

and usually drive herself to the restaurant. If she didn't have a date she'd ask Darren, the KP chef, to make her a small salad or some such. In the afternoon she was always busy, with phone calls to the boys, perhaps a therapy session, and other personal things to catch up with. Or she might surf the TV channels, flick through glossy magazines or pick up the phone to contact friends . . . Before the divorce she knew the Kensington Palace switchboard monitored her calls, but for some reason she blithely—and wrongly—imagined afterwards, when the switchboard was no more, that if she used her mobile her calls would remain private.

Sometimes there would be a memorably relaxed evening with friends. I remember one Saturday night in 1996 in particular, for it was the first time I met Diana's friend Richard Kay. I'd gone to KP with Ursula, a friend both of mine and Diana, armed with the makings of supper. While it was cooking Ursula went to the loo, and seconds after she emerged about six policemen stormed into the kitchen and then went into Keystone Kops mode as they made certain that all was well. Ursula, it seemed, had pressed the panic button in the loo instead of the light switch. The police left soon after that and we all shrieked with laughter about the whole incident. Richard had to leave some time before midnight but Ursula and I stayed on. At one point Diana remarked what a lovely comfortable evening she was having, when even the small silences were companionable. 'Just a Saturday night in with the girls,' I told her before Ursula and I left, tired and still giggling about our brush with the law.

By 1996 I was going to Kensington Palace so frequently—sometimes as often as five times a week— that I felt quite at home there. Certainly the security blokes just waved me through the gates with a grin. I really enjoyed those hours in Diana's sitting room, softly lit, scented with cinnamon candles and incense from China or Japan, and comfortable with deep sofas and the music always low and soothing. There were many warm and funny evenings. On the night of the 'security alert', for instance, we had gone to KP after Diana had suggested supper there. When she rang I'd asked her if there was any food in her kitchen and she'd answered vaguely that there was plenty of salad stuff. Any pasta? I asked. Don't think so, she replied. So I brought fresh pasta and the makings of a nice tomato-based sauce and set about things in the kitchen soon after my arrival. Diana leaned against the kitchen units, apparently fascinated as I went about the routine tasks of chopping and slicing, making a dressing for the salad and boiling water for the pasta. This was the most simple of meals, but Diana watched the quick preparations as though I were performing some extraordinary feat of culinary excellence. It was as if she'd never seen anyone prepare and cook a meal before.

While I was cooking curiosity got the better of me and I peeped into her cupboards. There were stacks of packets of pasta there—one of her favourite foods, but Diana clearly didn't know it was there. But in any case, she didn't yet have a clue about how to cook this easiest and plainest of dishes. Perhaps she learned something as she watched me in her kitchen that evening, and thereby stretched her repertoire beyond toasted cheese, sandwiches, baked potatoes and tea. Certainly she later grew more proficient in using the microwave and called me once in a frenzy of pride and delight after she'd 'cooked', for the first time, a ready-prepared pasta meal in it. I hope she never repeated the mistake of offering her famous bacon sandwiches to a small group of Pakistani friends whom she'd invited over—the microwaved pasta would have been a much better bet.

I smoked when I felt like it and there was always white wine in her fridge for anyone who wanted a glass or two. I don't know how anyone got the idea that Diana was prissy about things like that. She didn't smoke herself, and rarely drank, preferring fruit or vegetable juices and herbal teas, but she wanted her friends to relax and was never censorious about the traditional social unwinders.

After one of those rather silly, long and chatty evenings I left in the small hours, forgetting how poor my night vision is. I drove straight over the lawn outside Diana's front door, and will never forget the sight of the Princess running outside in her socks and laughing at me. 'Where are you going?' she called. 'You're in the middle of my front lawn!'—a fact which I hadn't noticed until she pointed it out. I believe the grass recovered but after that, if it was going to be a late evening, she would often insist I took a black cab home on the KP account. Her concern was no doubt as much for the flowers and shrubs outside her door as for me, but her kindness and consideration were no less real for that.

Perhaps it wasn't so strange that Diana had asked me to cleanse and heal her part of Kensington Palace of negative energy after her official separation from Prince Charles in 1992.

The palace is an enormous and remarkable building, its complexity really only understood by a study of aerial photographs. The remodelled building was completed in 1696 by Sir Christopher Wren after William III had bought Nottingham House, the original Jacobean mansion which formed the core of Wren's work, seven years earlier. While many of Britain's royals retained happy memories of the place—including Princess Victoria who was born in the palace and spent much of her childhood there, aware that it was her destiny to become Queen—other ghosts may not have been quite so benign. In 1702 William III was brought there to die after a fall from his horse, George II died there on his water closet, and during the Second World War the palace was hit and damaged by incendiary bombs. Not for the first time the 'Aunt Heap' fell into disrepair. By the time the newly refurbished Apartments Eight and Nine became home to the Prince and Princess of Wales in 1981, however, former glories had been restored along with the installation of the best of modern amenities.

In Britain the word 'apartment' generally evokes the idea of a spacious and luxurious flat. In Kensington Palace terms, however, it describes a very large complex of gloriously proportioned and appointed rooms, often on more than one floor, and set within beautifully tended grounds on the western edge of one of London's great central parks. Like any family, affectionate though they may be most of the time, the idea that a kind of Christmassy togetherness should be maintained throughout the royal family all year round is unrealistic, so a measure of privacy for each household is important. Apartments are therefore arranged to provide a modicum of privacy for the principal occupant, with security, separate entrances and little walled private courts and garden areas. In short, Kensington Palace is one of the most desirable addresses in the world.

Although Diana was later to make her own mark on

her part of the palace, which, despite everything, she continued to regard as home, in the first place Charles's taste dominated. He ensured that some of the palace's very best pictures, from a collection that included works by Rubens, Van Dyck and John Martin, should adorn their walls. Furniture, both heavily classical and impractically delicate, was arranged in the beautifully proportioned rooms with more of an eye to display than comfort. After the separation Diana did not consign all these great pictures and pieces to storage, but as soon as she was free to do so she introduced aspects of her own softer, feminine and witty tastes while managing to make many of the museum pieces fit in as well.

Given my interest in art, on the first occasion I went to Kensington Palace I was so overwhelmed by all the wonderful, if formal, paintings that I barely noticed anything else. My sense of the apartments' colours and style only struck me later and gradually. In any case, I had been invited, that first time, to deal with negative invisible energies in these rooms, not as a tourist or design consultant, nor quite yet as a friend.

Security was efficient but informal: so long as the guard's quick check confirmed that one was expected there was a wave-through and that was that. If I went home in a black cab I'd usually get a cheeky grilling from the driver, keen to hear some palace gossip—invariably without success, in my case.

That first time I was shown in by Diana's butler, Paul Burrell, who was impeccably polite, quite correctly not showing any informality. In those days Paul still wore the traditional brass-buttoned butler's uniform. Later Diana would happily agree to him wearing a good formal dark suit instead; indeed, before the designer's murder Diana

had been considering asking Gianni Versace to create a
new look for all her staff. That day Paul poured the tea
and then left, leaving Diana to take over. Tea was served
in those dainty little cups that contain only two swallows
and so, as a serious drinker of the stuff, I asked if I could
have mine in a mug. Paul was called to fetch one and the
tension eased a little—no one had made such a request
before. Soon I felt sufficiently calm to ask if I could
smoke. There were ashtrays around, after all, proper
large smoker's ashtrays and not those tiny little dishes so
often grudgingly provided in non-smoking households.
In due course I realized that, as so many of Diana's
friends and family smoked cigarettes, she was used to,
and completely tolerant of, the habit even though she
never lit up herself.

I have at home a round, aquamarine-coloured ashtray
which Diana gave me as a 'souvenir' after one of her
stays at the K Club in Barbuda. I believe there are a
number of others around town: Diana told me with a
twinkle that the porter at the club had remarked, as he
handled her luggage during one departure, that her bags
seemed to have put on a little weight since she arrived.
She also admitted to me that she'd considered 'liberating'
one of the club's luxurious towelling bathrobes, until she
noticed that they had an integral magnetic strip which
would have triggered an alarm if anyone had tried to take
one. There were also K Club soaps, matches and sta-
tionery in Diana's swag-bag after that Christmas of
1996. Best of all, for me there was a lovely sarong—not a
club freebie—aptly printed with the legend 'Even Para-
dise Has a Telephone'.

I have to take some responsibility for this habit of
Diana's. One day I went to KP directly after a book

launch at a hotel in Central London. In the ladies' loo there was a big jar of those little cotton-wool balls you use for fixing make-up or whatever. I grabbed a handful, stuffed them in my handbag and set off for Kensington Palace. Later, as I rummaged for my cigarettes, some of the little balls spilled out. Diana was curious so I explained. They're free, I exclaimed, when she looked doubtful. Jokingly, she chose to pretend that she thought it was theft and called to Paul Burrell that he'd better check the silver before I left. After that she became quite keen on collecting the occasional small souvenir from her own hotel stays, hence part of her collection of ashtrays.

That first afternoon I was seated on a sofa, one of two near the hearth in a drawing room which seemed to me to be to be bigger than a tennis court. A fire was laid but unlit, the winter chill countered by effective central heating. We chatted in our tiny pocket of that vast room for a while until it was time for the job in hand.

Given Diana's previous existence at KP I'm not surprised that she had a strong desire, after her separation and then, later, her divorce, to obliterate lingering, residual atmospheres. Except for her sitting room with its sophisticated music system, concealed TV and displays of her own treasures, the place was more of a gilded cage than a home. There were Prince of Wales triple-feather motifs on carpets, cushions, wallpapers and everywhere else where they could be reasonably displayed. Diana had deferred to Charles in almost every aspect of their domestic arrangements, and had followed the style of most royal ladies before her even in matters that were supposed to be within her domain, such as supervision of the kitchen and mealtimes.

Diana and I raced from room to room, all nineteen of

them (we did not make the roof terrace), the Princess having simply instructed me to work in whatever way I felt to be appropriate. I sensed a huge amount of negative energy in some areas, even a little in her relatively small and cosy private sitting room. Interestingly, this, like all her private rooms, was warmed by radiators or convector heaters. There was actually a beautiful old fireplace surround fronted by a starkly white, metal modern heater, before which lay the giant, squashy stuffed hippo (very comfortable for leaning and lounging, but not quite the same as the warm flicker of flames), facing a sofa. I asked Diana why she never had a real fire and she replied that it would create too much dust for such a small room—with so many framed photographs and ornaments, cleaning would have become a nightmare. I must also suppose that the feng shui expert she later called in saw no need to suggest the introduction of such a fire. Besides, her times with the boys in that room could not have been warmer or more loving.

There was the residual masculinity of wood and leather in Charles's former study, coupled with a general pervading sense of obstruction. The boys' rooms seemed fairly normal to me—William's mainly blue and Harry's yellow—except that they were unnervingly tidy for the bolt-holes of little boys, as was their own shared den. But I suppose the daily cleaning by Filipino maids helped, that and the fact that the boys were only there to sprawl about and generate messy youthful energies every few weekends and during school holidays. Diana's bedroom, all light and frilled and pastel and white, was a little-girl's room but also that of a very feminine woman, although the fluffy toys and scatter cushions on a chaise longue gave it a slightly incongruous air. It was here, where the

bed linen was changed three times a week, that she sometimes took lovers, but during those first KP visits I knew
nothing of any of this.

In the limited time available on that first day I had done
my best, but because of the rush I'll never be sure if I was
able to cleanse the place of all its old oppressions. It was
characteristic of Diana that afternoon, however, that she
thought everything, even intuitive work like mine, could be
done fast. In other contexts the slow, sometimes grinding,
wheels of any kind of bureaucracy perplexed her and, tragically, she was never to learn that things worth achieving
usually take work and time. As I've said, after my cleansing
efforts she had some parts of the apartments at Kensington
Palace feng shui-ed, as well as comprehensively redecorated
to her taste. Maybe Diana wasn't leaving anything to
chance, or wanted another specialist to deal with corners of
the apartment that I'd missed. I didn't mind, as I have the
greatest respect for the ancient Chinese art of placement. It
helps people to become harmonious with their home or
office by carefully looking at the arrangement of key aspects like windows, doorways, mirrors, beds, light and heat
sources. Perhaps the thousands of people who rearrange
their furniture, apparently out of random, bored impulse,
are unconsciously obeying the spirit principles of feng shui.

In any case, Diana's home was to become a much
lighter place in every respect, so I think I made quite a
good start for her.

During her marriage Diana was offered, every Monday
morning, a selection of choices for that week's menus,
planned to last the whole week until Friday lunch. Then a
similar Highgrove routine would swing into operation for
the weekend. While she was free to choose from options
within those menus there was little room for real self-

expression, and formal mealtimes were strictly adhered to. I have often wondered whether some of the eating disorders from which she suffered during her marriage sprang from the fact that, having overseen the food planning, she had little anticipatory interest in what would ultimately appear on her plate. For some dieters the very thought of food creates salivation and appetite, but many others who wish to lose weight will testify that appetite can be stifled and dulled by the vicarious 'eating' of illustrated recipes. Chefs who pay particular attention to presentation of their dishes know well that we eat and savour with our eyes as well as our tastebuds. The deadly, leaden knowledge that a certain formal dish was due to be served at a specified time might well have caused Diana to yearn occasionally for a simple snack when her body clock called for nourishment of a different kind and at a particular moment. During the years of her marriage, however, the Kensington Palace kitchens weren't geared to cope with the eccentricities of anyone's 'midnight munchies', or any other food craving for that matter.

Dinner parties when the couple were still together tended to end early—well before midnight—for both were early risers. But I know from my experience of evenings with Diana that while she usually went to bed at a sensible time, there'd be other evenings when she wanted to sit up and talk and nibble much later into the night . . .

Nor, during her marriage, did she always welcome being woken at seven in the morning on the dot, even if it was with a large cup of her favourite strong coffee. She was usually expected to hurry to the shower and dress properly to join her husband at the table for breakfast. This was seldom a leisurely affair as Charles would be keen to get to his office and Diana, of course, wanted to be ready to take her boys to school. Small children do indeed need their routines and Diana would never have let Princes William and Harry down. But this almost regimented system would not have suited someone who might occasionally have wanted to be a little more spontaneous and—in another life—sometimes to have thrown a coat over her nightdress and driven her sons to school while munching the last of her toast.

Even off-duty, ostensibly free evenings during their marriage were scarcely less structured if Charles and Diana were alone at home together. It's not hard to imagine how a spirited young woman, who had known a few accepted modern freedoms before her marriage yet who performed all her official engagements with a studied dedication which passed as panache, would sometimes long for things to loosen and lighten up.

During her short and tantalizing taste of freedom before her marriage, Diana had a number of part-time jobs that still left her plenty of time to shop and gossip and lunch, and to enjoy evenings which were blissfully free and unstructured. As far as I was later to see, she had not forgotten the few lessons about housework she had learned in those days (one of those jobs had been as a cleaner to her sister). I believe she and her flatmates had a cleaner to deal with the worst jobs, but Diana rather enjoyed some household chores like ironing and, especially, washing up. In all the years I knew her she didn't trust any maid to clean her own bathroom as thoroughly as she could do it herself, rubber gloves cheerfully pulled on for the task. And she preferred to hand-wash her lingerie and underwear rather than trust such delicate items to the palace laundry service.

Her perfectionism and need for personal order may

have been subconsciously expressed in 1992 when, speaking with acute retrospective self-insight about the time before her engagement, she told Andrew Morton, then preparing his book *Diana, Her True Story*, 'I knew I had to keep myself tidy for what lay ahead.' She was speaking of her chosen lack of sexual experience, but anyone who uses such a phrase in this context must have desires for order and control so strong that they border on fear of any threat of chaos. Sometimes these rigorous standards would baffle staff at Kensington Palace, for their intense loyalty to the Boss and enjoyment of informal chats with her in the KP kitchen could be challenged by a sudden burst of criticism if some small domestic task had not been performed swiftly and with exactitude.

Long before I knew her Diana certainly enjoyed ironing as she watched the soaps on TV. You see a *result* with ironing, something crumpled, if not actually chaotic, is smoothed back into order ... I believe that, given time, she would have developed other household management skills. Mercurial lapses of calm good humour if a staff member occasionally slipped up would probably have become less common, too, as she came to understand better the frustrations of certain domestic tasks. So thrilled was Diana by her eventual mastery of the microwave in her small private kitchen that I would not have been surprised if she had ventured beyond convenience 'cooking' and learned how to roast a chicken herself, rather than simply give the bird to the main kitchen staff downstairs to deal with, as she did once when I gave her one.

By 1996 Diana was becoming very interested in matters organic, so I went to a specialist poulterer and

bought a chicken, which I handed to the Princess when I
visited her, saying it was a little present. She peeped inside
the bag and burst out laughing. No one, she said, delight-
edly, had ever given her a chicken before. I explained it
was organic and suggested that it might make a nice meal
for the boys, who were at home that weekend. Diana
could not have been more pleased if I'd presented her
with a bracelet from Asprey. She didn't have the faintest
idea how to cook the chicken, of course, and Paul's help
was called for, but that sort of informal gesture really
pleased her. I suppose it reminded her of the life she had
never really had time to get used to when she was living
with three great friends in her flat only a mile or so
away from Kensington Palace in sunny, simple, single
South Ken. Then there was that night when she watched,
fascinated, as I chopped lettuce and vegetables and
made a dressing for a salad. Diana, who still thought that
all salads were bought ready-prepared in cellophane-
wrapped packets, might soon have been preparing them
for herself.

Already she was a dab hand with the juicer and was always keen to experiment with new combinations of
health-giving vegetables: carrot juice in the morning as a
wake-up, a mixture of celery and cucumber juices to
combat water retention, and beetroot juice to bolster the
immune system. But the vegetables *had* to be organic.
Diana came out in hives if chemically fertilized vegetables were used and a quick dash to Planet Organic in
Westbourne Grove for supplies of the real thing would be
called for.

As a young unmarried woman living in London Diana
hadn't needed to use her cordon bleu skills much. Most
evenings she and her financially cosseted girlfriends went

out for relatively cheap and cheerful suppers together or with groups of innocently gallant young men friends. But before you could shake a duvet Diana was transported to a world where dirty dishes washed themselves up and a trip to a supermarket was an occasional novel adventure, not a weekly practical necessity. Her slender grasp—and tolerance—of domestic realities would all too easily have slackened. Thus it was that her pride in making the perfect bacon sandwich was so great, and just about matched by her ignorance of the functions of gadgets in the kitchen and the foodstuffs left for her in the larder.

Much of whatever little she had once known had been obliterated by the hurricane of her induction into the royal family. Almost as soon as her engagement was announced she was scooped off to Clarence House, the residence of the Queen Mother. Diana was reported as being unsettled by the steady, beady and not entirely affectionate gaze of her future grandmother-in-law, a lady whose devotion to Prince Charles is well known. 'The Queen Mother drives a wedge between Diana and the others,' one of the Princess's friends was later to tell Andrew Morton. 'As a result she makes every excuse to avoid her.' Diana said much the same to me.

Released from at least some of her royal shackles and free again in Kensington Palace, Diana could still appear to forget that once upon a time she had briefly lived in the real world. She used to tell me, without dissembling, I swear, but with astonished delight, that taxi drivers would take you anywhere for nothing more than an autograph. 'Of course they would,' I told her, 'since it's you, Diana, Princess of Wales.' Somehow she had forgotten that in the outside world people carried money in their pockets and purses as she had once done. Little things like that made me wonder what other aspects of reality had been siphoned away from her young understanding when, early in 1981, she began her basic training as Princess of Wales. Retrospectively, words about poor little lambs who have lost their way—innocent, sacrificial and destined for slaughter—cross the mind. However, the training Diana received before her marriage was never intended to equip her for a life alone. For that to have been an aspect of that unique training course would have been unthinkable—in fact, impossible.

So it wasn't really Diana's fault that she was so hopeless about money. Since her marriage she'd never had any real instruction about its value, she'd never had to carry cash, and she was endlessly sent or offered things as gifts. The cab drivers who were honoured to have her as a non-paying 'fare' were not very different from the restaurateurs who discreetly waived their bills, the florists, jewellers, dressmakers and designers who were very happy to be able to suggest that—without a royal warrant as such—the Princess had appreciated their wares or services, especially if she wore or used something of theirs in public. Only after her divorce from Prince Charles in 1996 did Diana begin to show a faint glimmer of understanding about the market cost of things. Then, mindful that from her admittedly substantial divorce settlement she would be obliged to meet certain household expenses which she had been spared before, she started to become as careful as any householder about careless purchases, wastefully blazing light bulbs and so on.

Diana's divorce settlement was indeed considerable, especially when hidden 'perks' such as her home at KP, every aspect of the upkeep of her boys and other subsidies are remembered. After long and painful discussion she had walked away with a sum vastly greater than that which her sister-in-law, Sarah, Duchess of York, had been awarded when she and Prince Andrew divorced. Diana was angry on Fergie's behalf about this, believing that it illustrated yet again how expert the former 'in-laws', as she called them, were at graciously accepting assets, but how slow and unwilling they could be in meeting financial obligations of their own. She encouraged Fergie to renegotiate and fight for more. Certainly even Diana's divorce settlement, compared with that of Sally Croker-Poole, the former English fashion model who married the Aga Khan in the 1960s, was almost paltry. The Begum cleared over £50 million, a palace on the shores of a Swiss lake and jewellery valuable enough to underwrite a small national debt.

Diana and I were meeting and talking often during the year before her divorce, when the stress she felt was predictably high. My slight shyness with her diminished and then very quickly vanished altogether. Equally, her trust in me increased. She was still experimenting with many different forms of therapy, and seemed to want to learn from me so that she could offer healing herself. But during those spring and summer months I saw Diana becoming even more tense and assumed responsibility for her well-being correspondingly keenly. 'Cold turkey' is an ugly phrase often casually used to describe the pain that addictive people endure as they strip away dependencies and learn to live without their props. As a therapy junkie Diana was going through something akin to this, even as she had to shoulder new blows. By early 1996 the lawyers were arguing about custody of the boys, visitation rights, their educations, and countless other aspects of the divorce, and there always seemed to be some new piece of troubling news about Charles and Camilla to cope with. Diana's self-esteem was drooping. Yet she stepped up her public engagements, hoping, I'm sure, that by offering help and hope to others she could ease her own pain.

Once she had learned how to bring down healing energies from a universal but unseen source and to focus this strength, she began to transmit it through her hands to disadvantaged people she met through her work. She was particularly sensitive to children she met during both formal and unscheduled hospital visits and to the homeless for whom, ironically, she had a particular affinity, since she, too, believed that she didn't quite belong anywhere. She always felt especially bleak at Christmas. The season reminded her of her mother's departure and since the young princes were always away with their father and the rest of the royal family at Christmas, Diana felt terribly alone inside the beautiful but cheerless prison of Kensington Palace. I could relate to this, since my family have spent Christmas abroad for as long as I can remember; as a result I have established a Christmas tradition of my own by inviting to my home all the people I know who would otherwise be by themselves. At Christmas in 1994 I asked Diana to join us. I think she considered the offer seriously before declining, preferring instead to visit homeless people in London hostels for the second year running. In 1996 she went to the West Indies and called me on Christmas Day, her voice brave with the cheer and relief of an escapee.

Perhaps the nearest Diana came to enjoying a traditional Christmas celebration in the years before her death, amidst people who felt true friendship and affection for her, was when, also in 1996, she hosted a party for her Kensington Palace staff. She'd planned for this to take place at London's Planet Hollywood restaurant but some logistical problem messed things up at the last moment. Diana made a call to a friend, a very pleasant private dining room was arranged, the menu was sorted out, and the party was a huge success. The dining room was at Harrods, and the friend who obliged during the Christmas rush was the store's owner, Mohamed al-Fayed. Diana, a hugely valued customer and regular shopper at Harrods, was well placed to ask such a favour, especially as her stepmother, Raine, was on the Harrods board.

That year Diana gave me a glorious hand-painted silk scarf for Christmas. It really is beautiful, but I'm not a 'scarfy' person and knew, truthfully, that I would never wear it. I sheepishly admitted this to her and she was quite unconcerned, suggesting that I should frame it instead. A few days later when I dropped off some presents at KP she presented me with an enormous Fortnum & Mason hamper of exotic fruits, knowing that my very favourite presents are usually edible. The fruit lasted well, but was gone in the new year. The scarf remains, tissue-wrapped in its box.

She would have loved to have been closer to her own family. Her relationship with her mother was difficult, and when her brother Charles moved to South Africa contact with him became infrequent. She had been fond of Victoria, her brother's ethereal former wife, and they may well have discussed eating and weight disorders, both understanding from different perspectives how repelled Charles Spencer was by women who carried even ounces of superfluous flesh. But Victoria became off-limits to Diana after her brother and sister-in-law parted.

As a result the Princess's affections and loyalties were again divided, as they had been between her and her sister Jane, the wife of the Queen's private secretary, after Diana's troubles with Prince Charles emerged. She saw Sarah, her other sister, more often and with greater ease, but perhaps not often enough. Sarah lived in the country, so although they spoke every day, spontaneous visits were not easy. For someone who valued family ties so much, Diana saw precious little of her nearest and dearest.

The strained relationship with her mother, the delicacy of matters between her and her brother Charles—who had not complied with Diana's request for the use of a small house on the Spencer estate, Althorp, after her divorce—the troubled situation with her sister and Kensington Palace neighbour, Lady Jane Fellowes, and the fact that she saw too little of her other sister, Sarah, may explain why she took such an interest in my own family. In the mid-1990s, within a few months of my visits to Kensington Palace becoming frequent and regular, the Princess was to startle my own mother with an invitation to tea there. One Sunday afternoon when Diana and I were having some cucumber juice at the palace my mobile rang. It was my mother—by a curious coincidence also called Frances—who refused to believe where I was until Diana took the phone from me and said hallo. Mum was still unable to believe that this was the Princess of Wales and said 'How do I know it's you?' Diana immediately invited her to come for tea one day so that she could see for herself.

On the appointed day Mum had her hair done in the morning and dressed carefully before our taxi arrived. She had wrapped one of her own paintings for Diana, and had written a poem for her as well. Once we'd arrived at Kensington Palace Diana couldn't have been more charming to Mum or tried harder to put her at her ease. In the private sitting room where music was playing softly in the background they talked for over an hour about family matters and domestic practicalities—Mum remembers asking Diana about housework! 'She was like fresh flowers. Everything about her glowed—her eyes, skin, hair—and she moved like a dancer.' As she prepared to leave Mum asked Diana if she'd like to join our family for a meal in Hendon one day. 'I'd love to,' was the answer.

I think Mum will regret for the rest of her life that she never actually made a date for Diana to come. She thought about it and fretted because she didn't think the house was smart enough and wasn't sure if there were enough matching plates. I tried in vain to reassure her that Diana wouldn't be the least bit concerned about something so unimportant and that what would really matter to her would be to be amidst a real, loving, unpretentious family. Even so, their meeting is a memory that Mum will cherish for ever, along with the beautiful little enamelled box that Diana sent her, with a card, shortly afterwards. 'I saw this and thought of you,' was the Princess's simple and touching message.

By 1996 Diana was turning to me more and more, as someone whom she generally saw on a simple, private, one-to-one basis. At first our times together at KP would fly by in hours of chatter about trivialities: make-up and fashion, gossip about TV personalities, and such shallow matters as shopping and grooming. As time passed we'd speak more often about healing, about philosophical and spiritual things, and about our personal lives.

In time I felt able to confide in her about my worries, romantic, physical and domestic, as well. She always did her best to comfort me. One day in 1994 she found her bag of runes and the accompanying book of interpretations and gave me a reading. Not bad, either, for an amateur—although to be fair she had been reading her own rune stones long before I met her. She read my runes and looked at the cards to see what the future held, and in 1996 we regularly played an innocent predictive game together on the Osiris board I'd given her. This has a slightly mystic name but is no more or less than a harmless fortune-telling game, rather like the I Ching that has been intermittently popular down the years. Osiris boards are stocked by many specialist game stores and simply offer the amateur a jolly way to look into the future with friends. We asked the board about Prince Charles, her boys, Fergie and anyone else whose welfare was of concern to Diana. Although I have some expertise with it and would happily have given her a reading, had she wished, Diana emphatically didn't like the tarot because some of the pictures on the cards frightened her. Mainly, however, she had an almost childish excitement about and enthusiasm for these ways of seeking advice about the future and the handling of everyday life. Before their rift, she and Fergie used to leaf through magazines like *Prediction* and would sometimes call psychics—or 'spooks', as they always called them—who offered telephone consultations. Occasionally Diana would visit one of the seers who advertised, or whose work she had read about, arrangements being made by her office.

Without being conventionally religious, or indeed a regular churchgoer, Diana was certainly extremely spiritual and had her own strong faith in God and all the finest Christian principles. It is possible that at one point she may have been considering converting to Roman Catholicism, like the Duchess of Kent, although it should be noted, in the light of speculation at the time, that this is not the same as even being rumoured to have taken instruction. A little later she might equally well have toyed with the idea of becoming a Buddhist. She took a serious interest in all the world's great religious paths and had studied the Koran as well as the Bible. I don't believe that, at the time of her death, Diana was any closer to becoming a Muslim than this, despite speculation regarding her attachment to Dodi Fayed. When we talked of matters of faith we broadly agreed that no formalized religion could be as important in God's eyes as kindness and decency in thought, word and deed, and that a true believer doesn't need to go to church to pray.

She had, at last, made Kensington Palace her home. By 1994 many of the rooms were seldom used and retained much of their formality. But a few, her own and those where she and the boys slept, ate and entertained their friends, bore her mark, and she could relax in these pockets like any well-heeled single mother whose divorce settlement has included a remarkably comfortable, pleasant family home. Those cold, grand rooms lay only yards but almost a world away from Diana's private ones, linked to them by a short passage and a plain door. When occasion or duty demanded she would fling open the heavy double doors of the splendid function rooms in welcome. And then she would sparkle in the expected way, as Princess of Wales. But I'm sure her few true friends preferred the different, quieter glow she displayed when she was in the handful of rooms she felt to be truly her own. I felt privileged to be able to share this private space with her.

4

Princess Perfect: The Boss

When Diana was displeased there was no mistaking it. Like all of us she lost her temper sometimes, and the explosions weren't always logical. People under stress often appear to endure extraordinary pressures, only to react with quite inappropriate fury if a tap drips, a dog barks or a cup breaks. Such stored and misdirected rage is always the most frightening because its victim will seldom have defence mechanisms mustered, particularly if the angry person has previously seemed easy-going and calmly tolerant of life's smaller complexities.

Furthermore, she was, by 1996, becoming increasingly mistrustful of anyone she felt might be taking advantage of her or violating her rules of absolute loyalty and discretion. Her suspicions had whittled down the numbers of people whom she felt she could safely regard as friends. Many fell by the wayside at some stage and stalked the Diana wilderness, often baffled about their 'crime', until she was ready to summon them back. Others were never recalled, as though she had ruthlessly decided to strip certain people out of her life for ever. For a few former friends or members of her staff who had been particularly supportive of the Princess during her darkest times, this cutting, blanking severance was particularly upsetting.

Her angers were often, though by no means invariably, short-lived, but friendships that endured did not do so unscathed. She was furious with her friend Mara Berni, who co-owned San Lorenzo, Diana's favourite Knightsbridge restaurant, when Mara alerted the press after she'd invited her friend to attend the opening of her new dress shop. Diana's feeling that she had been used was perhaps rather naive, as was her failure to realize that the paparazzi were bound to be there. In any case, she gave Mara very short shrift for a time, although after this brief faltering of trust their friendship resumed. She also fell out with the Duchess of York, who had been, perhaps, her greatest friend, and there were even tense times with Richard Kay, the *Daily Mail* journalist with whom she had established deep trust over the years.

For some time Diana had been more than willing to allow Richard to draft and polish her public speeches. He knew her so well and understood her natural vocabulary and speaking rhythms so acutely that he was able, with her co-operation, to prepare many a public statement for which she would thank him later. But in 1996, just before her divorce, when Diana became especially concerned about her image and as a result wished to be more concise in her public statements, she decided that Richard's draft speeches were too long and complicated. Martin Bashir, who interviewed her for the famous *Panorama* broadcast in November 1995, offered to draft her speeches in future. Richard was dreadfully upset, although he did not withdraw his affection for the Princess and remained a friend, despite his hurt. I had reason to sympathize with him, but I was also pleased to see that

Diana could make her own choices and stand up for herself. Part of her late growing-up would inevitably involve some mistakes. As it was, her friendship with Richard weathered the upset.

A clutch of other friends also survived temporary exile. Some, like Rosa Monckton and Angela Serota, weathered all potential storms and stood loyal and firm. But others, including Carolyn Bartholomew and her contemporaries from those flat-sharing days, were not to be rehabilitated after they fell from grace. Many of the friends at Diana's funeral had not seen the Princess for years. The invitations had been dispatched on the basis of names found in an outdated address book or some old Christmas card lists . . .

For many of her former friends there was never to be time for the considered, two-step dance of Diana's *preferred* method of reconciliation. When she was ready, and not before, she might metaphorically crook her little finger in the direction of her social Siberia and summon the offender back to her tiny inner circle. In the meantime, such outcasts may well have tormented themselves about what exactly they might have done to deserve their punishment, raking over their memory of Diana's emotional minefields and wondering which unintentional blunder or remark could have breached the peace. Once restored to favour, no reference would be made to the 'crime' which had precipitated the exclusion of the still-baffled but now rehabilitated friend.

As Diana had gained, with painful irony, some control—almost empowerment—over most aspects of her life, so by 1996 she had rather come to relish her power. Early in her marriage that power was self-directed, used to control her weight and redesign her body. Now she rather liked to sit down, as it were, at an invisible chessboard and move her human pawns about, with long pauses between moves if it suited her. Whenever I had to stand by and watch as Diana beckoned exiled friends back into her most intimate circle, I wished that she could achieve this without resorting to this cat-and-mouse game of blanking then beckoning back.

The trouble for anyone around Diana was that she—and they—were all victims of her need to control. She loved the idea, the fantasy, of her team at Kensington Palace all pulling together, so that her staff were lulled into the notion that here was some kind of first-names egalitarian family. This was, however, something of an illusion. Anyone who failed to recognize that there was stern stuff behind the Princess's apparently informal, even jokey, wish to be known as 'the Boss' was risking a very rude awakening.

Sometimes Diana's tantrums were expressed by sudden ballistic rages—for instance, if her wardrobe was not organized just so. This, as I've said, was confusing and unnerving for staff who had served her diligently for years and had come to imagine that the Boss would tolerate a rare lapse in the precise ordering and folding of her blouses and shirts. The painful task of telling a staff member that they were dismissed fell to Paul Burrell.

At other times Diana's anger would be expressed in an even more distressing way—the baffling, silent freeze-out. A member of staff may have dusted a photograph frame or ornament but simply failed to replace it in precisely the same place to experience a very cold shoulder for such extremely minor incompetence. If crimes like this rattled Diana's fragile equilibrium once too often, the culprit would be blanked.

The staff member might only realize that they had offended in some way when the previously warm and unstuffy employer who had appeared to take a genuine interest in their lives, and even in their families, failed to show even the merest flicker of recognition when next they saw her. Even her most loyal and trusted staff could be misjudged if Diana fell victim to these mercurial tendencies and adopted a black-mooded view about insurrection in the house. At one time she even formed the ridiculous idea that Paul—a man who would have laid down his life for her, as I pointed out to her at the time—was untrustworthy and she briefly considered dismissing him. That Paul remained with her, despite her period of stand-offishness, speaks volumes for his loyalty, affection and understanding. The same must be said, too, of other staff who stayed (despite KP's notoriously low wages, even after Diana had raised them), when they too fell briefly out of favour.

This sort of thing undoubtedly created tensions at Kensington Palace and sometimes made it a mixed blessing to be there, for me, sensitive to atmospheres as I am, as well as for staff. Pressures could build upon Diana until quite a small displeasure could be expressed by an inappropriate rage, she crying with anger about some outside slight coupled with the lightest of KP last straws. I pitied whoever it was in the firing line that day. To be fair, this sort of crisis became increasingly rare, but staff who stayed on knew how easily the Princess *could* ignite.

That Diana felt physically ill during these dark moods obviously didn't make things any easier. Anger would knot her stomach so that she couldn't eat and stress invariably manifested itself in back and shoulder pains.

These would sometimes respond to relaxation exercises, and she still saw a therapist for this specific problem. Like most women Diana suffered from pre-menstrual tension so things around her were more likely to become volatile at certain times of the month. She had been taking the pill for years to ease this syndrome, but it didn't take all the aches or moodiness away.

These thundery moods didn't show in the way she dressed, nor did she let off steam in careless or aggressive driving. Usually a skilled and careful driver, during the time I knew Diana she had one minor accident in London, caused by a momentary lapse of concentration, and no one was hurt. I suspected that it wasn't the first, however. After that she briefly lost her nerve and used a driver for a few weeks. But missing the freedom of jumping into her own car soon had her back behind the wheel. Another time when she witnessed a road accident she dashed over to see if she could help and, unrecognized, slipped back to her own car where she alerted the emergency services on her mobile.

In a black mood, Diana might play music more loudly—always classical or opera—and this seemed to calm her. It amuses me mildly that people associate her with pop music. She liked it well enough, and was certainly friendly with a number of pop luminaries, especially George Michael, Elton John and Cliff Richard. One afternoon in 1995 she invited Take That for tea at KP. Reporting back, she said they were nice, polite, young men from Manchester and felt flattered when one of them asked her on a date. She had to turn him down, but he was, she said, terribly understanding. But the music that she preferred and played at home, whether she was by herself or with friends, was invariably classical. Although she was moderately accomplished, she rarely played the piano herself when alone, but she often turned to CDs of the gentle, calming Chopin *études* or Schubert pieces she had played as a girl. When I gave her a CD of ballet music she said, with a wistful, faraway look, that Tchaikovsky always reminded her of Prince Charles.

Sometimes a particularly strenuous workout at the gym would enable Diana simultaneously to deal with her anger and give her a physical-exercise 'high'. Running at night also helped. She would pull on some jogging pants and trainers, place a sweatband low over her forehead and take to the quiet back streets of Kensington and Knightsbridge, often speaking into her mobile phone as she ran. No security officers monitored her and I was always worried about those runs, even though I knew that they helped her to defuse frustrations and tensions. People get mugged just for their phones, I warned her, but she wouldn't listen.

If her tantrums and moodiness, as well as her disregard for her personal safety, brought problems for her staff, they faced another in that Diana quite often thought she could do their jobs better than they could. While this may seem trivial, it is actually quite a telling facet of her character. As I've said, before her marriage she had had a number of little jobs cleaning, ironing, bath-scrubbing and floor-polishing for her sister and for families of friends. No doubt she was treated warmly by her employers as a social equal rather than as a skivvy, with the result that she had regarded these jobs as work to be both enjoyed and done well before driving home to her flat. The big difference between the young Diana and most other house-cleaners, however, is that, changed after work, she was likely to set off for some kind of dinner date with friends of the friends whose houses she had been cheerfully cleaning earlier.

Diana didn't have so many recognized achievements to her name before her marriage to have forgotten later that she had once been a Duchess of the loo or a Squeezy Queen in the kitchen. When I knew her she had her own pair of rubber gloves for doing the washing-up, a 'chore' (if it can be called that in her case) she particularly enjoyed. As well as knowing how to iron properly, how to dust and polish, nobody could clean her bathroom as well as she. Every tile was carefully polished—particularly after a bath steeped in aromatic oils, which could leave a slightly greasy film on bathroom surfaces—and every mirror gleamed. She was also fussy about her white clothes, and laundered them herself, with dazzling results: I never saw her in a T-shirt, blouse or pair of shorts that was even slightly tinged with cream, grey or any other shade. Sometimes she even cleaned her own shoes.

Incidentally, whilst not being in Imelda Marcos's league where footwear was concerned, Diana was very fussy about her shoes and when she found a style that she liked she would buy more than one pair, often in a range of colours. The same sometimes went for things like dresses and T-shirts. This practice revealed both her confidence in her own taste—a knowledge that she would still like something enough to want to wear it even after it was really worn out—and a form of insecurity. Just as people who have starved will sometimes eat frantically because they fear that they may never see food again, so Diana was stockpiling against the risk that this or that item of clothing might not be available in the future.

Inevitably, Diana's exacting household standards unnerved some of her staff and sometimes actually caused them to slip up now and again, especially if they had been coaxed into the illusion that the informal, unmade-up Princess who sometimes padded about Kensington Palace barefoot in leggings was just one of the girls . . . It is true that double standards did underpin Diana's home life. Her wish to be liked was very finely balanced with her wish to be respected and, indeed, indulged or obeyed. That same paradox underpinned many of her other relationships— notably those with her friends, the press, and some professional associates.

A curious incident struck me as being emblematic of Diana's new ability to control things, coupled perversely with a mischievous respect for the forces which control us. An admirer gave her an amethyst—not a rough-hewn crystal, but a beautifully square-cut stone that might have been set into a ring or a necklace. The Princess, however, felt that it contained bad energy. Perhaps she wasn't especially fond of the donor, or perhaps she simply didn't like the translucent violet colour of the gem, or even considered it to be unlucky. In any case, she decided to bury it in the soil of an orchid growing inside KP. She was both gratified and horrified to see that the orchid died within two days. Retrieving the amethyst, she then buried it somewhere in her small, private area in Kensington Gardens. Truthfully, I don't think she worried much about whether or not the unlucky stone was going to affect some other plant life.

Although cynics might have seen her passion for cleaning as an aspect of Diana a little like that of Marie-Antoinette playing at being a simple shepherdess at the Petit Trianon in the grounds of Versailles, they would have been wrong. When Diana got her hands dirty in the sink she was scrubbing and cleansing and 'making things better' in just as serious a way as she was when she got her feet dirty and risked her life during foreign missions abroad. She was proving to herself—and to critics in government or Fleet Street as well as to dissidents among her own ranks of staff and supporters—that she had standards that she would maintain at all costs.

Her 'hands-on' approach extended to her work with charities. Diana had, undeniably, rather liked her figurehead status with many of the organizations with which she was connected, and had been sorry to relinquish some of these responsibilities when she so dramatically reduced her commitments. But her main concern had always been the work actually accomplished by those charities. She scrutinized their accounts very carefully and wanted to know how their money was used, becoming very displeased if she thought that directors of 'her' charities were disproportionately well paid.

Naturally Diana's staff at Kensington Palace could not have been expected to interpret her mixed messages with total accuracy all the time, and nor could they have known the details of her personal stresses. But they may sometimes have been unsettled if, albeit rarely, they overheard a distressed Princess curse and swear during private phone calls, although she always controlled her language with her staff. Resorting to profanity at times is only human, and if her employees really imagined that she was a kind of goddess far above such human outbursts, they were swiftly disabused of the idea if they happened to pass the door of a room in which she might be making a particularly upsetting call. All in all, working for Diana at Kensington Palace, with its constant worries about committing an 'unforgivably' incompetent act, was not easy. Nor was it conducive to a serene environment.

But if Diana was on a short fuse, it must be remembered that the pressures upon her were enormous, and that the public mask was very seldom allowed to slip. The fact that she was the victim of her own charisma and success did not make this any easier for her to bear: everyone knows that it is usually simpler to find someone else to blame if things go wrong than to accept personal responsibility. Apart from the one time, early in our friendship, when she apologized to me, admitting that she had been wrong to ignore my advice concerning her friendship with Oliver Hoare, I don't think I ever once heard Diana say 'I'm sorry.' Not to me, nor to anyone or about anything else—except in the relatively trivial context of apologizing for telephoning at a bad time or for some other minor inconvenience. The Diana I knew, riddled with insecurities as she was, needed to recover self-esteem before she could find the courage and confidence to accept her fair share of blame when something that mattered to her went wrong. In the two years since 1994 therapies had taught her to try to release her unresolved angers and pains, old and new, but until shortly before her death she wasn't yet ready to do so with proper and appropriate control. She knew by then that to internalize them could be damaging to her. She had seen enough therapists to know that a childhood marked by unexpressed hurts and fears of further abandonment was something she had to address and work through, rather than relive. She was in a delicate specific stage of personal growth when I met her, and just trying to learn to deal with hurt. Given what she had contended with, Diana made extraordinary leaps of emotional progress during the years I knew her, but occasional lapses could make the progress jerky, sometimes seemingly two steps back for every one forward.

Quite often, someone who has plunged to their physical and emotional depths but who has subsequently recovered will be embarrassed to be with people who even saw them at the low points, let alone those who actually helped to restore them. It's as if those supportive people, associated as they are with the worst of times, are thought to bring bad luck or, worse, to give the lie to a newly found strength. As a healer I've encountered this rather unappealing aspect of human nature many times: the back is turned and the shoulder cold as the healed and restored person moves on, stepping away from the very people to whom they partially owe their recovery.

Diana was not often like that—at least, not for a long time.

So many things had caused her pain. As an example, she had regarded Princess Margaret as a staunch friend within the royal family until she received a wounding and excoriating letter from her after the *Panorama* broadcast, which left her feeling abandoned once more. That the next stage for her was to understand and deal with her angers was actually healthy for Diana but often difficult for those around her.

Sometimes she could express veiled displeasure in a deceptively relaxed, even mischievous way, although I was aware that at such times her behaviour was not always as playful as it might seem. She had, for instance, little affection for her Kensington Palace neighbour, Princess Michael of Kent: the Christmas cards exchanged between them each year just about expressed the strength and depth of their neighbourly and cousinly regard. Once when I visited Diana at the palace I waited in the

dining room while she concluded a meeting in her office.
There was a scratching at the window and I looked up to
see an adorable little Burmese cat on the sill. Paul was
there and I asked him to let the cat in. She came to me at
once—cats have strange knacks: they instinctively know
who likes them, and also recognize cat-haters and will
jump on them out of spite. I come into the first category
and was happily stroking the little Burmese when Diana
entered the room.

She laughed and said that the cat belonged to Princess
Michael, but often lurked around her own apartments. She
then mischievously suggested that I took the gratifyingly
purring cat home with me. Although I was tempted, I knew
that I couldn't possibly do so; besides, the hovering Paul reminded Diana that Princess Michael had had her aristocratic cats equipped with a computer chip which would
make them easily traceable—and get me into some trouble.

The idea was quickly laughed off and the cat sent back
towards its nearby KP billet. But when I think of this
little incident, however innocent and good-humoured it
seemed at the time, I find it revealing about aspects of
Diana's residual resentment, bordering on rebellion,
towards anyone connected with the royal family, and
also about her ability to allow someone else to take the
blame if something went wrong.

My guess is that others took the flak when Diana almost ruined the Queen's seventieth birthday party in
1996, although the Princess might well have come under
suspicion. A private family dinner had been arranged at
one of London's smartest restaurants. Diana, who was at
the time annoyed by restrictions placed on her by Buckingham Palace, as well as delays to permission for her to
visit Angola and Bosnia, rang me gleefully to tell me of

her plans. I couldn't approve of them, but there was no stopping her. She alerted some members of the press about the venue. Carefully planned Palace arrangements had to be changed and although the dinner went ahead, what had been devised as a happy secret was spoiled by the last-minute panic and absence of surprise for Her Majesty. 'Do you want to hear something really funny?' Diana had asked me. 'I've tipped off the press!' It was another example of her continuing resentment of the royal family and many of those connected with it; indeed, she told me that she felt sorry for Sophie Rhys-Jones, Prince Edward's girlfriend, simply because Sophie was so deeply involved with what Diana called 'that family'.

This long-stifled anger was sometimes expressed in unexpected ways. Impulsive and impatient, Diana became rattled when things she wanted to happen *now* took time. She couldn't understand, for instance, why work she had committed herself to for the anti-landmines campaign in the months before her death took so long to organize. The seemingly endless series of meetings concerning this, at Kensington Palace and elsewhere, baffled and frustrated her. *She* had done all her homework and was ready to go. Why wasn't everyone else? But although she travelled to Angola and Bosnia in 1997 as a private citizen, a form of clearance for her, as Princess of Wales and mother of the future King, had to be obtained from Buckingham Palace, and this took time. The same frustrations applied to some of her work for other charities and causes.

The truth is that Diana had fiercely strong opinions about social issues, and felt an equally strong frustration that she had virtually no framework or forum in which to voice them. She was aware that many people thought she was merely a beautiful airhead, and that, maddeningly, some of her own ironic and self-disparaging remarks had contributed to this notion. Certainly she was expected to deplore third-world poverty or to make bland generalizations about the importance of parenting, but she also had strong, and at times controversial, opinions about contemporary issues and longed to express them.

I knew, for instance, that she was in favour of the death penalty for murder. The crimes of the serial murderer Frederick West in Gloucester reinforced these beliefs. Diana believed that forensic medicine is so advanced today that the danger of an innocent person being wrongly convicted was now infinitesimally small, and that society as a whole would be safer if the deterrent threat of capital punishment by hanging or lethal injection was reintroduced.

She believed, furthermore, that rapists should be castrated, that drunken drivers should be banned from the roads for life—this particular view was vehemently expressed to me after her mother, Frances, had been convicted of a driving offence—and that the victims of crime or their relatives should be properly compensated rather than the perpetrators who were so often expensively rehabilitated courtesy of the public purse, or worse, Diana thought, given money in compensation for 'unjust' prison sentences. She told me that she would happily sign any petition that proposed such legal reforms. In this she was almost certainly reflecting the views of many millions of the British public who share her belief that British 'justice' is soft and meted out unfairly. Every time Diana read of the mugging of a pensioner or inner-city burglary she bristled with rage about the way victims seemed to be given less consideration than 'underprivileged', and thus needy, offenders. Her views may have been oddly old-fashioned for a progressive princess, but she adhered to them passionately. She had no wishy-washy liberal tolerance for thugs and bullies of any class, colour or creed.

Diana spoke of such matters—among many others—with Tony Blair shortly before her death, as they attempted to plan together the national and international role for her that she so greatly desired and that the Prime Minister was so ready and willing to consider. He probably reminded her that despite the opinion of a great many of the public, the House of Commons was unlikely to pass legislation restoring the death penalty for murder, or, without great difficulty, to pass some of her other proposals, but at least now there was some serious dialogue for Diana at last.

Diana's views addressed extreme cases. To do her justice, she could be sympathetic towards the first-time offender or towards someone whose miserable circumstances or fragile mental health had led them to offend again. Wherever rehabilitation could help such people to recover, she was all for it; indeed, she thought that more should be done. But if someone repeatedly offended—whether their crime was murder, rape, violent theft or other serious abuse—Diana advocated the sort of punishment which would prevent them from ever hurting someone else again. She tended to agree with the principles of justice advocated in the Old Testament—'eye for eye, tooth for tooth'. She often spoke to me of a time and an age when people confidently left their back doors unlocked without fear of intrusion, and wished for a resumption of such simple, honest, trusting days.

* * *

With children, however, Diana never showed any sign of such impatience or of her short fuse, for she was always magically able to relate to each child at his or her level, to create a bond. Albeit with the help of her office, who reminded her of all their birthdays, Diana was loving and caring towards all of her many godchildren and remembered each of them in her will, and she was a dream of an aunt to all her sisters' and her brother's children. Her own sons inherited her sense of humour, including that love of practical jokes. Just as her dark moods could be unpredictable, the oddest things could make Diana laugh: she hooted when William impersonated his father rather than admonishing him for disrespect and once, after having seen a hedgehog on Hampstead Heath, she could barely control her mirth as she regaled me with a description of the creature, making it sound as though it were some massive, mythic beast that might belong in a sci-fi movie.

I'm not particularly sentimental about children, but even I could see that Diana's boys were both very likeable young men. William was endearingly protective towards his mother and strong for her in an almost adult way when she needed support most. He also used to chide her for wasting time and money on the telephone and had, as a fourteen-year-old in 1996, taken a very grown-up hand in the plans for the charity sale of some of her most spectacular formal dresses. Diana took his ribbing and Harry's occasional mischief with unconditional love and patience. For her boys, whenever she could have them for a weekend or during the school holidays, there were lots of hugs in front of the TV. Her times with them in that room, with its many ornaments and framed photographs and the giant, squashy stuffed hippo in front of the beautiful old fireplace, could not have been warmer or more loving.

If these were some of Diana's most private times, it has to be said that she was obsessed with the protection of her privacy. Although she could become effortlessly lofty and detached when it suited her, she was terrified that people might be abusing any private privilege. She could be almost paranoid about breach of trust, and if she gained the slightest notion that someone was exploiting a connection with her for personal gain or kudos they were cut off completely. Sometimes she was astute about this, but at others her fears were unfounded; as a result she severed good friendships for no good reason. Anyone who has had to trust entirely to their own judgements about such matters is bound to make mistakes, and Diana was no exception. Some of the things which enraged her were predictable. She was almost speechless with anger after Ruby Wax, whom Diana had believed to be a trusted friend, seemed to use the connection to become close to Fergie, the American comedienne thus being guilty, in Diana's eyes, of 'disloyalty'. It was a pity, for they had been great friends. Diana loved the other's sense of humour, and Ruby had often come to Kensington Palace, her own experience of life's problems helping her to advise the Princess.

Miss Wax had wanted to make one of her expertly intimate and revealing TV specials with Diana, intended to be a friendly and humorous exposé of her 'victim' and her home life. When Diana declined she had happily settled for a programme made with the arguably ill-advised Sarah, Duchess of York—with whom the presenter had by now also become the firmest of friends. Many who watched as Ruby Wax wandered through Sarah's home and peered into her cupboards thought that the Duchess was demeaning herself. Diana and Fergie were still close at the time but in 1996, even as she despaired of her sister-in-law, Diana was capable of having a wicked laugh about her now and again. Once, during a conversation in which Diana was muttering darkly about Sarah, I unthinkingly interjected with a good old East London expression which described the Duchess in rather less than flattering terms. Diana looked up blankly and I gathered my wits. There was a pause as the remark sunk in, and I thought I might have overstepped the mark. Then she released one of the loudest peals of laughter I've ever heard.

Diana's angers were slow and hard to dissolve, however. Moreover, she was so prepared to be instantly on her guard that she easily misread a situation, but then found it very difficult to admit that she had been hasty, judgemental, or plain wrong, let alone to apologize. Her sense of persecution often ran over to affect her view of what was written or said about her publicly. She would skim the newspapers and often pick up on some unfortunate phrase concerning her. Without reading the whole story, she would then be plunged into a pointless rage. At times she was so defensive that she'd assume that the world was out to criticize and misrepresent her. She would then ask offending journalists, as she perceived them, to come for a private lunch at Kensington Palace so that she could set the record straight, failing to understand that her previous—and often unsuccessful—attempts at manipulating other members of the press corps were well known, or that the thrill and pride a journalist might feel at such an invitation could not always buy trust or loyalty, or obliterate the memory of previous manipulations.

In fact, and despite a professed hatred of most reporters, Diana knew all about the power of the press, and at times she would flatter important journalists. She was delighted to accept an invitation to the *Sunday Times* Christmas party—I think it was in 1996—for instance. But she seemed unable to understand that favouritism and selective manipulation of journalists could backfire, and that if she played her hand badly she had only herself to blame. It is strange that whilst self-castigation loomed large in Diana's psychological agenda, she was, perversely, very slow to accept responsibility if things didn't go her way.

She had another silly row with Richard Kay before she died. It concerned a piece he'd written for the *Daily Mail* which she considered traitorous. She went ballistic, but in fact she had barely scanned the article, and had only picked up on certain words. As it happened, Richard was coming to my flat for supper that evening. He was terribly upset about Diana's reaction, thinking it meant the end of his friendship with her. She actually called while we were talking about it. I told her that Richard was with me but she wouldn't speak to him and asked me to call her back when he'd left. Having done my best to reassure Richard that all could be sorted out, I duly waited till he left before calling back.

Firstly I urged her to read the newspaper piece properly, and then I read it out loud to her. At last she was able to see that it was more than fair to her. Two days later she called Richard as if nothing had happened. Upset as he was, his ultimate loyalty did not falter. But

Diana was becoming headstrong in her recovery and sailing very close to the wind in several ways.

She had tried to boost the morale of one of her secretaries, Victoria Mendem, at Christmas in 1996. Separated from her boys, she escaped from Kensington Palace and flew to the West Indies on Christmas Eve, taking Victoria with her. Later I heard Diana's version of events. Victoria had known she was to be the Princess's companion for the stay and had expected to perform some secretarial and screening duties whilst they were away. These she accomplished with great tact, especially when a rich casual acquaintance of Diana's had tried to secure a mooring for his yacht at the nearest harbour on the— false—grounds that he was scheduled to visit her. Diana was outraged—it was another example of people trying to use her—but Victoria saw to it that the boat's owner and his guests did not come anywhere near their holiday apartment. Diana had called me from Barbuda to say that she could see this 'little boat' on the horizon. In the morning she woke to see a very large yacht. Victoria was also on constant stand-by for companionship. At that stage of the holiday Diana was still in reasonably good spirits, but perhaps a little bored and not having quite as much fun as she'd expected. Why else would she call me all the way from Barbuda simply to share a mildly amusing anecdote? During a brief cloudburst on an otherwise blazing day, three barefoot West Indian cleaners had respectfully walked through her suite wearing plastic macs and holding mops. It reminded Diana somehow of the comic duo Morecambe and Wise, she told me, howling with laughter.

There are at least two sides to every story: if Victoria was later surprised to learn that her employer expected her to pay for half the cost of her 'holiday', Diana was to tell me that she had found irksome Victoria's dietary restrictions and preference for a quiet time rather than fun diversions—paradoxical in a woman who had her share of dietary fads and who professed to dislike crowds. The truth is that Diana could only cope with the paparazzi, the crush of public attention, even a traffic jam, on *her* terms.

There was, however, a third side to this particular story, in that Victoria failed to make the right smokescreen phone calls a month later when the Princess wanted the press to gather outside the home of her former crush, Oliver Hoare, in expectation of discovering Diana resuming her former stalking tactics there. In fact Diana wanted to be free to go somewhere else entirely and without risk of observation. Victoria, it seems, became muddled by these complicated subterfuges and did not acquit herself to the Boss's satisfaction. In any case, she soon left her job at Kensington Palace.

I often wonder why Diana chose me as her friend, for she was hardly short of willing escorts and companions. It may be that she still felt she had to play a role in front of some of them, to hide her interests—from the most trivial and banal to some of the world's most serious ecological and social issues—in case she was ridiculed for either. Until her sister-in-law Sarah betrayed her, as Diana saw it, by talking about her while promoting her autobiography in the United States, Diana used to spend most of her Sundays with Fergie. It is a crying shame that the latter felt constrained to ignore Diana's pleadings to keep silent about her. A shame, too, that Diana then overlooked Fergie's good points, even though she knew that her behaviour over the book was driven by a desperate need to get out of a financial pit. Diana herself had often gently chided her sister-in-law for being over-generous to friends with cash as well as presents. She'd told Fergie that she should learn to budget, as she had done, and she'd encouraged her to renegotiate her divorce settlement. Even when she was at her most financially strapped Fergie continued to give presents, even if, like the expensive night sight for shooting she bought for Prince William, they cost a fortune.

Like me, Diana never had a fondness for blood sports. Not so her sons, however, who love to go hunting, shooting and occasionally fishing. As well as participating with their father, from time to time their uncle Charles, Diana's brother, would take them shooting on his estate at Althorp. So you can imagine William's delight when he received a night sight, worth £4,000, from Fergie at Christmas 1996. Diana, who was not speaking to her sister-in-law at that time, realized it was a ridiculously expensive gift from a woman still struggling to pay off her seven-figure overdraft. Fergie refused to take it back and told William that if he ever needed to talk to someone he should give her a call. Diana's response was typical: 'Don't you dare.'

Before this rift the two young women had too few genuine friends to be able to afford to lose even one of them. These two, friends long before their respective marriages and with so much in common, used to be able to relax, holiday and laugh together about things that few other people could possibly understand. Even though an abject Sarah made attempts to mend things after their row, writing notes and leaving phone messages, Diana maintained her silence, not yet ready to see Fergie as merely misled rather than unforgivable. Perhaps she should also have recalled the good nature with which Fergie had forgiven Prince William, as the victim of his practical jokes when the two women and their children had taken a villa in France one summer. Fergie and Diana were going out for the evening and the former had arranged for a hairdresser to come. The boys were sitting outside with Beatrice and Eugenie by the swimming pool. As Fergie bent down to kiss her girls goodnight, Prince William crept up behind her and threw her into the pool. At first she was furious, but then managed to see the funny side—just. On another occasion, Fergie came back to the villa late in the evening and all the children pretended to be asleep having turned the lights off and locked all the doors, so that she was forlornly knocking on the door well past midnight. William is a great practical joker and he often phoned people up pretending to be his father, whom he can mimic wonderfully well—just as his mother could mimic the Queen. Although, as I've said, she could often freeze people out, Diana usually thawed quite quickly. This, however, was an instance of her remaining aloof and inflexible: she was never able to trust Fergie again after that violation of her privacy.

Diana was very close to Sir James Goldsmith's wife, Annabel, and all the Goldsmith family and began to spend her Sundays with them after the rift with Fergie. I think Annabel was a mother substitute for Diana, the Princess's relationship with Frances Shand Kydd remaining very delicate and subject to new cracks for every old one that seemed to be mended. One of the last and most hurtful of these came only a short time before Diana's death, when Frances told *Hello!* magazine that she was pleased that her daughter had been stripped of her HRH status. Diana saw this as an act of spite and malicious jealousy, and the latest in a short but devastating series of betrayals since she had first realized despairingly that her marriage was doomed.

Diana admired the way Annabel Goldsmith had seemed to place the importance of a continuing family life above all other considerations, and marvelled at her ability to remain with the late Sir James despite being well aware of his infidelities. After those Sunday lunches, which, according to Diana, though cheerful affairs, were utterly dominated by Goldsmith, she and Annabel would walk in the garden, talking quietly. She trusted the older woman absolutely, and I can only surmise that at times she might have wished that she had been able to relax with and confide in her own mother in a similar way.

Diana had become very friendly with the photographer Terence Donovan and his wife. When Terence took his own life in 1997, the Princess was not only caring towards and supportive of his widow, also named Diana, but anxious to do all she could to shield her from rumours which, after his death, circulated about her husband's infidelities.

Conversely, she could be impatient sometimes if she felt friends were draining her and yet taking no notice of her advice. Once when I was at Kensington Palace I picked up a call from Lady Cosima Somerset, whose private life was complicated at the time. Diana felt that she had given enough of her time and energies without getting much emotional support back and signalled to me to tell Lady Cosima that she was not at home.

But in the main Diana almost always welcomed opportunities to meet someone for a private lunch if that friend had problems and Diana believed she could be consoling. She wanted to walk into walls and pits of pain, public or private, to forget her own crisis for a little while as she strove to understand someone else's. It was a form of displacement activity, and one that I watched and despaired of. She had arrived at this alarming point because it was easier to try to deal with other people's problems than face her own at this supremely delicate time. It was relatively easy to cloak this stage of her personal growth with a concern for others which effectively forbade potentially dangerous questions about herself. As a result, Diana became an expert in *friendliness*, but was sometimes too cautious to be that very different thing, a friend. Sincere friendship which she had offered in the past was not always reciprocated when she needed it most. She even felt upset and let down when her close friend Rosa Monckton demonstrated that she had other priorities, even though, as godmother to Rosa's daughter, who has Down's syndrome, Diana must have had some inkling of the pressures on her friend.

Again sadly, the real affection which Diana felt for Prince Andrew also came under threat because of his family's attitude towards her. It would have been doubly hard for Andrew to be publicly friendly with Diana when she had fallen out with Sarah as well as with the rest of his family. It was excruciating for her when, as the mother of William and Harry, but otherwise excluded from the inner family circle, Diana had to attend official royal functions looking radiant and happy yet knowing herself to be surrounded by hostile, or, at best, ambiguous vibrations. Without even Andrew's tacit, almost brotherly, support and understanding, this discomfort was made all the worse.

Added to all this, Diana was usually obliged to be circumspect with society friends who mixed in the same circles as her estranged husband and his family. For some or all of these reasons, therefore, she had reached out to an improbable person like me for friendship, and also for confirmation that her growing interest in healing and complementary medicine was to be taken seriously rather than dismissed. Everything I have ever read or heard, and continue to read and hear, about Diana being fickle and using or abandoning friends angers and upsets me. Friendship which works is always a two-way business, and even if she could sometimes be demanding she paid back, in her own way and in spades. The Princess was a woman to whom friendship was very important—she needed friends more than most. Yet this was the area in which Diana displayed some of her most troubling paradoxes. She simply hadn't had the joy of enough real friendship in her life to be able to discern between a disagreement and a chasm, a lull and an end. Towards the end of her life, confidence restored but delusions, it must be said, also creeping in, she took this to extremes— assuming that the 'offender' would always be ready to step back into her little circle demanding no explanation, let alone apology. As we have seen, Kensington Palace staff often bore the brunt when her patience snapped and she came to imagine that her friendly manner was being abused and that she was being watched, rather than *watched over* in the protective sense. Offenders there could be excluded or replaced fairly ruthlessly, as friends could be at times. It may seem to be an irony that such 'betrayals', as she saw them, only happened because she was so open and trusting in the first place. Now I see it rather differently: however much she might have liked to believe otherwise, I don't think Diana was quite ready to offer, or accept, complete trust.

A curious thing happened after Diana's father died in

1992 which, while it utterly belies the widely held view that she seldom forgot a grudge, also in fact demonstrates that she was as inconsistent in this respect as she was in many other areas of her life. The tactful intervention of a third party could often persuade her to think again about someone she might have misjudged. The vignette also supports another, rather deeper study of her character and illustrates her strong drive for reconciliation and order in family life. As a child Diana had, along with her sisters and brother, referred to her stepmother Raine, the former Countess of Dartmouth, as 'Acid Raine'; indeed, the children used to chant 'Raine, Raine, go away' in response to their father's remarriage. For years there appeared to be little or no evidence of real affection on any side. And yet when Raine was widowed (and perhaps when Diana had finally given up hope of establishing a close relationship with her own mother, Frances) the two began to meet in London regularly, at least once a week, often for tea at the Ritz or some other comfortably discreet place, although Raine seldom came to Kensington Palace. Diana was alone amongst her siblings in attempting here to construct a family bridge where once there had only been a chasm of hostility. Knowledge, if not understanding, of this counterbalances something of the lingering image of Diana as an intransigent woman unless her immediate family or favourite causes were involved. She was clearly hoping to resolve and then shed some pointless emotional baggage and move forward in a spirit of understanding and friendship.

Diana's friendships with people in the world of show business were undoubtedly real, but seldom if ever could she invite Elton John, George Michael, Wayne Sleep *et al.* over to Kensington Palace for a relaxed and informal evening. She felt, with them, that she too had to be a star and so she would usually see them at glittering occasions when she showed only her most stylish and glamorous sides. Actually, I think all her friends from that world would have felt even more honoured to see her as truly relaxed as I so often did.

That Diana genuinely appreciated and enjoyed the company of artistic and musical gay men has sometimes been misunderstood. She wasn't, like the late Princess Marina, her distant aunt by marriage, what is known as a 'fag hag'—a woman who is most at ease in the safely bloodless company of distinguished homosexual men. Marina's 'walkers' included Sir Malcolm Sargent, Sir Noël Coward and Danny Kaye, men who willingly and charmingly escorted her on numerous occasions, essentially as social accessories. By contrast Diana's affection for George Michael, Elton John, Gianni Versace *et al.* was a simpler expression of admiration for their work and an innocent liking for the trappings of celebrity. I'm sure it was entirely reciprocated, although even these friendships were not entirely immune to her caprices.

Vague angers and resentments are usually harder to deal with than an unmistakable affront. Gianni Versace had been one of Diana's favourite designers and also her friend. Just before he was murdered in the spring of 1997, and shortly before her own death, she had agreed to endorse a book about his work, partly because proceeds were to go to an Aids charity. She hadn't realized until she checked the proofs, however, that the final edition was to include photographs of naked men as well as formal and rather beautiful pictures of some members of the royal family. As soon as Diana realized this she publicly withdrew her support for the book and the whole enterprise.

Versace sent her flowers in the hopes of easing the situation, but their mutual friend Elton John was not to be so easily mollified. His manager, John Reid, wrote Diana a letter on the angry side of chiding after he learned of her withdrawal, as he saw it, from the greater cause.

It was yet another example of Diana testing a true friendship—and she had few enough of those. On that occasion she really had been placed in an impossible position. For me it was particularly poignant that she and Elton John were able to kiss and bury their differences at Versace's funeral shortly afterwards. Only weeks later the singer delivered his 'Candle in the Wind' tribute to Diana at her own funeral service in Westminster Abbey. By great good fortune, as it turned out, he and the Princess had managed to repair their friendship before Diana's light was snuffed out. I was not to be so lucky, for we quarrelled some months before her death.

It was time for her to be free of me, although I only see this clearly now. At the time I thought that a little of her old damage had resurfaced and that she wasn't willing to let me help her deal with it. But as we'd quarrelled before and had always been reconciled I wasn't too distressed. But time passed and soon it was high summer. In August 1997 I took Rachel, my sister, on holiday, and just got on with my life and work, expecting that all would work out. I've always been an optimist.

The news of Diana's friendship with Dodi Fayed was splashed over every newspaper and on the TV news each day. My many messages and notes to her continued to be ignored, but I thought 'Good for you, girl. You deserve some happiness.' I never saw her again.

5

That TV Interview

For a very long time Diana had trusted the Duchess of York; indeed, she had regarded her as her best friend, much more than a sister-in-law. But, as I've said, Fergie irrevocably upset Diana over her autobiography—I remember that the telephone call went: 'Fergie—it's your show, you're the star. Please don't talk about me any more on American TV'—and neither woman could have known that there was never to be time for a reconciliation.

She was, however, still very close to Fergie during the period before she was interviewed by Martin Bashir for the momentous BBC *Panorama* programme in November 1995. Fergie wasn't the Princess's only adviser about this—I understand that Diana's brother, Charles, also encouraged her to go ahead with the interview—but she was certainly hugely influential. In a television interview with Jonathan Dimbleby a few months earlier, Prince Charles had spoken about, among other things, his long-established affair with Camilla Parker Bowles, and it was natural that an upset and humiliated Diana would want to have her say. For myself, I felt that it would have been infinitely preferable if she had maintained a lofty and disdainful silence. Watching that programme, I thought that Diana seemed almost to have lost her mind and attempted to pull a vulgar stunt worthy of Fergie herself in those days. I told her so forcibly: to have described that interview as something of a disaster would have been an understatement. In the event, Diana's public support, albeit briefly, crumbled and melted so badly after the interview was broadcast that soon afterwards she told the world that she was stepping away from the centre stage of public life.

We'd not been in touch for a short while before the *Panorama* broadcast. Diana had exasperated me by insisting I saw her at a particular time when I was already committed to treating an elderly and disabled woman whose schedules could not be tampered with. Diana wasn't happy about this but I wouldn't budge, refusing to give her preferential treatment. I actually thought it might be good for her to realize that she couldn't always have things her own way, even—or perhaps especially—amongst her small group of intimates. Still largely surrounded by sycophants, she had yet to learn that friendship is founded upon give and take.

I had watched the *Panorama* programme in a palsy of fascination and horror. The Princess's appearance alone was shocking: the hair seemed too stiff and bleached, the face and lips too pale and the eyes rimmed too heavily with black. As I remarked to her at the time, all this, along with the funereal dark suit, evoked, for me as for many other commentators, nothing so much as the image of the murderer Myra Hindley that haunts the British consciousness. Although Diana's voice was low and at times faltering, the honesty of her words was somehow countered by the coy lowering of her darkened lids as she simultaneously looked up from beneath them, showing the whites of those stricken eyes. This was art-directed, stage-managed 'sincerity'. Having already confided so much off-camera to

Martin Bashir, Diana was, if not exactly rehearsed, at least well prepared for the careful, sensitive questions which generated her dynamite responses.

In passing, I was interested to see similarities in the art direction when Louise Woodward, the English nanny convicted in the United States of manslaughter in 1997, was interviewed by Martin Bashir for BBC Television shortly after her return home in June 1998. Just like Diana, Louise sat in a dark suit, hands resting in her lap, with pale make-up and highlighted hair. I couldn't help feeling that this was deliberate manipulation of another young woman in turmoil—at emotional breaking-point, even—however calm and poised the youthful nanny may have appeared to be.

It was also plain to many people who watched the Diana interview that a misguided revenge was taking place. It was her turn to admit to having committed adultery, and her chance, as she saw it, to plead for a new role for herself in future. It is ironic that her wish to be seen as 'Queen of Hearts', since she admitted that she could no longer visualize herself as Queen in the future, misfired so dramatically when the public reaction to the programme was less positive than Diana had hoped.

Initially, I thought it was deeply and dreadfully beneath her dignity for Diana to speak of her relationship with and past love for James Hewitt. The man had betrayed her publicly by describing details of a relationship she had known to be illicit but believed to be private, in a book which became one of the most sensational kiss-and-tell stories of the century, and a bestseller. She felt violated and abused. Few could blame her for spoiling to fight back, even if she was entering the ring from a rather dirty corner. It is, however, only fair to remember that

Diana had had to bear her grief and rage in secrecy and silence and that perhaps she needed to air it at last. A public display of bereavement is, after all, considered in many societies to be a natural stage of the healing process when one has lost a loved one and Diana had never been allowed this. So however misjudged and misguided they were, I don't believe that her remarks about Hewitt were simply a sulky tit-for-tat revenge against Prince Charles.

We should also realize that within their own chattering circles the relationship between Diana and James Hewitt was observed and discussed. It may not have been boldly publicized in the newspapers, but plenty of people *knew* of the affair and the pressure upon both of them was mounting. All this is not entirely dissimilar to the situation in the 1930s when British 'society' knew about, and the foreign press both knew about and reported, the relationship between the Prince of Wales—later, if briefly, King Edward VIII—and Mrs Simpson. It was really only the 'common people' of Britain, akin to today's tabloid readers, who were rather patronizingly shielded from upper-class common knowledge by the government's muzzling of Fleet Street.

I understand that when Hewitt's book, *Princess in Love*, written with Anna Pasternak, was published Diana would barely speak of it. I met her soon afterwards and she was undoubtedly unwilling to discuss the hurts she still felt after a relationship which had mattered to her for three years. But burying hurt and anger is seldom a good idea, as the poet William Blake knew:

> I was angry with my friend
> I told my wrath, my wrath did end.
> I was angry with my foe:
> I told it not, my wrath did grow.

In retrospect I can see all sides of this, and so can regret neither the harsh way in which I criticized Diana for mentioning the affair in the *Panorama* programme—let alone for allowing herself to be pressurized into taking part at all—nor her need to express her pain so publicly. We can all be wiser with hindsight and the fact is that Hewitt's book, a second betrayal so painfully soon after her glum acceptance of her husband's affair, devastated Diana, upset her elder son and—she felt—diminished her. It was only human that she broke silence. If she also unwittingly shot herself in her elegant foot, that was part of the price *she* had to pay for *her* deal.

While it would be untrue to suggest, as some have, that Diana was completely duped about the intended nature of the programme, it is also untrue that it was shot over time with her hair and make-up carefully adjusted to make it appear a single continuous interview. True, she vetted the questions, and had her chance to consider how she would field them. There were also rehearsals, but the whole interview was filmed in one session. Various people have been credited—or have allowed themselves to be credited—with feeding her the most memorable lines: Ruby Wax, for example, is reported to have claimed that the remark 'There were three people in this marriage' was borrowed from her. This may well be true, as Diana and Ruby were friendly at that time and the wit, truthfully, smacks more of the latter than the former. Oddly enough, I always thought that Diana's phrase about her wish to become 'Queen of Hearts' was too slick for her, and that she might have been primed to use it by someone else.

Not only did the Princess, during that interview, scupper any residual hopes she might have had that her marriage could be saved—it was immediately after the programme's transmission that the Queen decided that enough was enough and that divorce proceedings must begin—but she briefly lost some of the public popularity which she had enjoyed before. Some of her hitherto adoring supporters stepped back for a while. The press were also very critical of her, and her ambition to have some sort of ambassadorial role in the world was not only questioned but ridiculed by some. Diana, so trustingly accustomed to a pretty unqualified sympathy vote, was shocked and startled: she had taken her revenge and pushed something off her chest, but she could never have expected that in doing so she might lose her sure grasp on the public's affections. It would be a little while before she won it all back. Ironically, given that her expressed desire to fulfil some serious international role on Britain's behalf had been mocked, it was largely through her independently organized work against antipersonnel landmines that she regained all that temporarily reduced public affection and regard, and won an enormous new global respect.

Shortly after the interview had been transmitted Diana decided to retreat from public life and lick her wounds. She did this, with typical caprice, in a terrifically public way during a short statement which was so widely reported that it was effectively a broadcast to the nation and, ultimately, to the world. Scores of charities would lose her official patronage and commitment. There would be fewer balls and galas, fewer official engagements and fewer photo calls. But the love she received from ordinary people was an energy which flowed with Diana's blood, and public interest in her didn't really ebb very far or for very long when she stepped back a little—as she was clever enough to anticipate. She needed that love, breathed it like oxygen, and couldn't live without it.

In the spring of 1996—and, I thought, very unfairly—
Diana was criticized for allowing herself to be filmed
during her attendance at and notional participation in a
major heart operation at the Brompton Hospital in London. Some commentators made snide 'What's-all-this-
about-retirement-from-the-media-gaze?' remarks. Those
large, clear eyes were indeed well made-up above the surgical mask, but her involvement in the operation was
cruelly misunderstood. She knew very well that her presence would attract publicity and this is exactly what she
had intended—publicity for Sir Magdi Yacoub's vital
and then underfunded cardiac foundation. Yet had she
attempted to make this clear through journalistic contacts it might, in the climate of early 1996, have been
misinterpreted as blowing her own trumpet. So again she
was constrained to remain silent.

When I spoke to Diana a week or two after the
Panorama programme I told her how misadvised she had
been. I felt rather brutal because she was already depressed
enough by the general reaction to it, although I was touched
that she'd found the courage to try to sort things out with
me, the disagreement over my promise to see someone else
one day in 1995 when she'd hoped I could meet her forgotten. I started going over to Kensington Palace again
soon afterwards. Diana seemed to have taken two steps
back since the last time I'd seen her, baffled and hurt by the
public response to the broadcast; increasingly she relied on
me for 'street' feedback. As her friend, I longed to cherish
and comfort her, and to tell her that she should have a
'what-the-hell' attitude to fickle public opinion. But I also
believed that I owed it to her to be honest. Frightened, worried and still a little imperious, she was aggressive and defensive all at once. It took a little time to re-establish trust.

Our initial conversations after that reconciliation weren't easy because I had to tell her that I believed the TV people had subtly pressurized her into participating. She was no more under obligation to go into the national confessional box than any of the rest of us, and I believe it was wrong for others to encourage someone as vulnerable, wounded and confused as Diana to do so. Anyone who suggests that she knowingly and completely willingly collaborated in the programme, and was pleased to have a vastly public opportunity to tell her side of the story, both misunderstands her and underestimates her naivety. I think the fact that her brother Charles, in whom she had such depths of trust, had suggested that it might be a good idea influenced her decision. Charles had come to know Martin Bashir through a business arrangement and thought that his sister's interests would be well protected by the interviewer. Beyond that, however, years of flattery and public adulation had convinced Diana, on one level, that she was perfect, invincible and in full control of her life. The irony is that she was as frightened and insecure as any worriedly guilty or misjudged child, and before the *Panorama* cameras as blinded and defenceless as a rabbit in the glare of headlights.

Nor had she properly considered the feelings of her sons and, retrospectively, was anguished about the effect upon them that her programme might have had. She hoped that Prince Harry was too young to have been fully aware of the meaning of much of what she said, but she had to deal with William's deep hurt and dismay. After the separation she had leaned on her eldest son very heavily. He is a very bright boy, astute and perceptive, and I remember her remarking that he had the wisdom of a sixty-year-old. Nevertheless, one of the few ructions between Diana and William came after the *Panorama* interview as a result of her having acknowledged her love affair with Captain James Hewitt. William went berserk after watching the programme at Kensington Palace, slamming the sitting-room door and refusing to speak to his mother for several days. Diana was absolutely horrified, the incident bringing home to her how much she had hurt her sons by her candour. No one had warned her to anticipate this or any other kind of criticism if she went ahead with the broadcast.

This, then, was the mentally bruised and confused creature I met again soon after the *Panorama* broadcast. And this, too, was the exhausted young woman who had somehow, soon afterwards, to overcome her frailty and deal with one of the most complicated British divorces of the century.

My heart went out to her. I worried that my bluntness might make things worse, but I was also certain that this would be the most effective way for me to help her. As I have mentioned, soon after the television programme the Queen had insisted that divorce proceedings should begin. As battle commenced Diana needed all her strength, with the result that she relied more than ever on her therapists for practical advice. Her greatest concern was for her sons and her priority was to ensure that, their educations permitting, she could see them in Kensington Palace, their own home, as often as was natural and proper. She also wanted to argue for her right to work as her own woman. The Palace, however, refused to allow her to earn a conventional living in future, so that she had to fight for a financial settlement that would provide for her sons and compensate her for the outrage of being denied the right to support herself and her family by her own efforts.

Offers flooded in from TV companies after the *Panorama* programme was screened—she could have hosted chat shows, fronted documentaries, even acted. She could have gone into business. Two major international media magnates, Rupert Murdoch and Kerry Packer, made her serious offers. She was very attracted by one proposal, in which she was offered a large sum to make half a dozen programmes about her charities. As a competitive woman, Diana saw this as a way of beating the money that Fergie was raking in from her own TV ventures. But if none of these proposals interested her sufficiently, Diana *did* want to work, and to do something worthwhile. She recognized, moreover, that she had the 'pulling power' to achieve much and resented the royal family's imposed restrictions. I think her husband's family and advisers were worried that whatever Diana chose to do might upstage Charles. Nor, despite speculation to the contrary, did she really care a fig when she learned that being stripped of her HRH status was to be part of the deal when her settlement was agreed. She was confident enough, if perhaps only just, to see this as the smallest of her concerns.

Yet she tested herself fiercely during this period when the divorce was being negotiated, and afterwards. Late in 1996, after her divorce, I sometimes went with her to an acupuncturist in Camden Town. I agreed with Diana that these treatments can be wonderfully effective, and she was also keen to learn about the philosophies behind Chinese medicine, healing which she recommended to many world leaders. We were seen in adjacent rooms with open doors and called out to one another and chatted away as the needles were inserted. My tolerance of pain is shamefully low and I would often cry out if a needle was slid into a sensitive spot, although I knew the benefits would be well worth the short splinter of agony. Diana, however, would only—and very occasionally—draw breath or gasp.

'How can you stand the pain?' I asked her afterwards.

'You forget, I'm used to it,' she replied—with a grin. She did admit that sometimes at night she would tug out the short needles which the acupuncturist had left in her ears, although they were meant to stay in place for five days, so even she had a pain threshold. I wonder if Diana was testing herself and that, rather than punishing herself as some might suggest, she was simply seeing how much she could endure.

For the sake of my own pride and the value I placed on our friendship I was naturally pleased that Diana and I were close again. But although I knew she was being very brave and coping remarkably well with the new levels of stress to which the divorce negotiations subjected her, I worried about her. Like anyone undergoing fearsome pressure she could behave erratically—as her staff and friends had come to learn. Only her sons were spared the inconsistencies sometimes generated by her mercurial moods.

As I struggled to cope with my father's death, she would often come up to North London, and our walks there on Hampstead Heath and our talks helped me a lot. Even though I was in a state of typical bereaved anger and she had so much to confront, I could see how much stronger Diana was than when I had first met her. Only in simple conversation and by her actual presence did she use her own growing healing powers with me, but by now she was gaining confidence in all of her abilities.

As battle over the divorce had commenced, she had needed all her strength, with the result that she relied more than ever on her many therapists for advice. She was, however, now far more ordered and positive about seeing them. I would no longer have described her as a therapy junkie because she was much surer about what she needed from each individual practitioner, whether that was relaxation or energy. And she was using her own healing gifts more thoughtfully by now. Had she lived, Diana would always have been highly strung and emotional, impulsive and probably too trusting. But by late 1996 she had learned to harness the positive aspects of all these qualities. She had become a free woman, and one with the means to take control of the rest of her life.

It is almost certainly no coincidence that at this time Diana was able to deal so well with yet another of the hand grenades hurled at her by a temporarily hostile press. At the time, it amazed me how dignified she remained in the face of all the speculation about her supposed affair with Will Carling, the England rugby captain, a story which had begun to dominate the press at around the time of the *Panorama* interview. The suggestions that she was some home-wrecking Jezebel must have hurt, especially as they were untrue. But perhaps I shouldn't have been surprised by Diana's calm because by then she was so much more self-confident, and no longer felt quite the same need to feed stories to friendly members of the press in order to have her side of things reported.

I watched Diana go through all this pressure and begin to soar. As her friend I felt pleasure and pride as I watched her in recovery. That pleasure was trebled when I began to see that the wounded person Diana had been was finding that she now had strength left over for others.

6

Searching for Happiness

Diana had one tiny injury that was to her a badge of honour. A little bump had appeared between the index finger and thumb of her right hand, testament to the thousands of hands which had shaken and often grasped hers as she went about her work. I expect every member of the royal family has one of those bumps—a kind of regal repetitive strain injury. Had there proved to be a long-term future for Diana I might have begun to worry, as bumps like that can herald arthritis. In the meantime, however, there were injuries which worried me much more.

The habit of self-wounding that Diana could descend to, even as late as 1994, was neither an indication of suicidal tendencies nor was it always a classic attention-seeking gesture. After all, almost no one saw the resultant scratches and scars, and she certainly didn't want to discuss with me the disturbing marks, bruises and lacerations which I noticed when she first began to speak to me of her miseries. They were private expressions of the rage, pain and frustration she felt at that time, but which her public position obliged her to hide. Having been in dark psychological places myself in the past, I could empathize silently with Diana, and she understood this. Eventually we were able to discuss things.

Diana's problem was one that is difficult to explain to people fortunate enough never to have been hurled, or even gradually driven, into that dark and hopeless pit. Sometimes mental pain is so extreme that it can manifest itself in torment as physically acute as that of a burst appendix, a severe migraine or the gut-wrenching cramps of colitis. Yet there is no fast and readily available painkiller known to man, woman or science that can alleviate this kind of agony. People suffering in this way may sometimes be so distressed that, in order to express their terrible yet invisible emotional pain, they will attack themselves. Since very often the person blames themself for the whole sorry situation they may, in their disturbed state, see this self-inflicted punishment as almost deserved. Somehow, they hope, the emotional pain will be released through a physical wound. And of course, however bravely and secretly such people, men or women, have been bearing their grief, they may long for the attention and concern that a visible wound will usually generate more easily than suppressed inner torture. This longing is, however, generally complicated by the simultaneous social need to conceal the evidence of wounding.

Diana was in the midst of such a conundrum when I first met her. I didn't realize until we began to confide as friends that those wounds were connected with her doomed friendship with Oliver Hoare. His patience had worn so thin that he had made public his concerns about Diana's obsessive telephoning, and her habit, even as late as 1995, of parking her car near his home and waiting for a glimpse of him. She had had to deal with this humiliation as well as everything else. The fact that it was just as illogical of her to have imagined that mutilating herself would bring Oliver Hoare to her side in a rush of loving pity and concern, as it had been before when she had hoped that similar attacks would regenerate Charles's affection, is beside the point. Or rather, it may actually *be* the point: no one as troubled as Diana was at either of these times can be expected to behave logically.

A child who has fallen and scraped a knee somehow realizes that if the little shock of the small accident is acknowledged with a kiss, a sweet, and a lovingly applied plaster or a bandage (far more elaborately administered by concerned and motherly hands than is strictly necessary), the slight tumble is soon forgotten. A different child, however, one whose injury is ignored and left to develop into a 'pull-yourself-together' scab, will pick at it, worsen it, sometimes infect it and, perhaps, never forgive the person to whom they cried out and ran trustingly towards. Being let down can become so frequent that expectation of it becomes a habit. And habits can become addictions.

Don't make a fuss was—and still is—a command often issued to English children of a certain class and generation. Being stoical is supposed to prepare them for life's later challenges. Young Diana had all the material privileges and advantages. But she felt she had been denied so much of the love and attention that childhood is supposed automatically to bestow—as a result, she did, belatedly, make a little fuss. When she found that her husband could offer her no comfort, she looked elsewhere.

Diana's first serious romantic entanglement during her marriage—with Captain James Hewitt of the Life Guards—came as a double-whammy. Even as her marriage was collapsing she imagined herself to have matured and become more sophisticated. She trusted that she could handle such a relationship with poise and competence. Here was a strong man, a soldier, someone Diana trusted to protect her. As a child she had formed a fear of horses after she had broken an arm when a pony threw her. Now she had found a man who could finally make her feel safe and confident when riding, bestow upon her one of the skills so prized by the royal family and which hitherto she had lacked—something she was sure they saw as failure and as a mark of inadequacy. Furthermore, Hewitt seemed to show her unconditional love even while her husband, as she was now so miserably certain, preferred the arms and attention of another woman.

Hewitt was tall, well spoken and handsome in a dull, knitting-pattern sort of way. The light informality of their lessons and her small subsequent equestrian achievements did much to bolster Diana's self-esteem. She was lonely, vulnerable and in dire need of a broad shoulder to weep on. She fell in love with him for these reasons and, perhaps, for the obvious sexual ones as well. The very qualities which attracted Diana to Hewitt made his subsequent betrayal of her all the more incomprehensible.

When they had decided to end their affair—due to the combined pressures of increasingly loud whisperings about the relationship and the threats to his career and her reputation having become too great—it had been with grace, fondness and dignity on both sides. Or so Diana had believed.

Perhaps later it was just too painful for her even to contemplate that idealized sort of man and the comfortable, relaxed country life that he might have provided, and which would have suited Diana rather more than the one in which she found herself caged. She could only discuss James Hewitt with me in terms of the disappointment, grief and pain she had felt, anguish which I tried to help her to cope with over the next couple of years. But although this was an assignment which I willingly undertook, it was not easily accomplished. So hurt was Diana that every nerve was raw; furthermore, she was in physical pain, especially in her neck, shoulders and stomach, however bravely she attempted to hide this when she made public appearances. Occasionally my sympathy wasn't enough and I had to recommend a therapist. She still took tablets sometimes to help her sleep, but only very occasionally would she take painkillers. Both of us believed that chemical cures should only be resorted to in desperation: sometimes Diana found them necessary.

The affair with Hewitt had been over for some little time when I first met Diana and she scarcely spoke of it, even after we became friends. But after the publication of the book Hewitt wrote with Anna Pasternak, *Princess In Love*, I knew as much about it all as any other tabloid reader. On coming to know Diana I saw at once how raw she remained and intuitively sensed how much that episode (and to a lesser extent her later infatuation with Oliver Hoare) contributed to the damage: many of her tensions and physical pains derived from crushing disappointment. For Diana, Hewitt's behaviour had crushed any hope she might have had of a gentle and civilized memory of an affair with a man she was to tell the world she had loved.

She had always expressed a wistful yearning for someone strong, stable and intelligent during the many 'if-only' fantasies we shared late in the evening at Kensington Palace. While she would occasionally admit to finding some TV-soap actor attractive—she told me that she agreed with Fergie that George Clooney of *ER* was 'hunky', and even feigned jealousy when the Duchess of York met the star in America—Diana mainly daydreamed of a loving husband who would not only care for her through any crisis, but who would accept her for what she was. She spoke longingly of a country life, preferably by the sea, of dreams of an old rectory or twee country cottage. For the Princess, however, the country could as easily have been France or America as England.

She had lost Charles and now, with this mess, her heart had been broken again too horribly fast for any mending to bolster her. Her trust had been abused and her spirit had almost perished, too. Her ragged nerves rendered it difficult to help Diana much at first: in expression of inner panic she was either stiffly over-controlled or too restless to concentrate on anything much. The blackcurrant pastilles she sucked on by the tinful brought only brief and temporary relaxation or relief. Nor do I know how she could have kept up her poised public persona if it had not been for her sons. Yet Diana had resources of inner strength that I doubt even she quite realized she possessed. Without this strength she would not have had the nerve—some would say recklessness—to embark upon one of the most extraordinary, almost quixotic, adventures of her life.

In late 1994 she was desperate for the return of her letters to Captain Hewitt and had made this plain to him. Within the royal family there persists a letter-writing culture—they tend to communicate with each other on paper rather than by telephone or by meeting to talk things over. For once Diana had fallen into their ways.

As any true gentleman would, Hewitt had promised to give Diana her letters back, but he suggested Spain as the place for the handover. Even though she was well aware that photocopies could easily have been taken she wanted to have the originals back—perhaps simply to deprive him of them but more probably because she feared he would sell them. I believe she would have burned them.

Hewitt called her from the Costa del Sol in Spain, suggesting that she meet him there to take possession of her precious letters. Diana was pitched into a state of miserable yet impulsive desperation. At some strange level she was, of course, excited, although she spoke of this only to me and one other, Susie Kassem, a discreet middle-aged friend, who was to arrange the tickets and travel with her. To avoid attention they would fly tourist class to southern Spain, Diana travelling as Frances Spencer, since she had a passport in that name which she had used before—I don't know where or why. Since it had a photograph of her in a short, dark blond bubble-cut wig Diana donned this for her flight to Spain, as well as carefully applying a toning make-up, darker than her usual one. She travelled, thus, incognito.

It wasn't the first time Diana had travelled or ventured away from home in disguise, but other excursions had been underpinned by a sense of adventure and a relishing of snatched, if not stolen, freedoms. This time, however, her heart was heavy, and beneath the mask of foundation and powder her face was set with a grim resolve. I'd seen that expression as the journey was planned.

Afterwards, while she did not exactly laugh about her 'mission impossible', she did say with rueful surprise that she didn't understand how anyone could bear to travel 'cattle class' on a long flight: she'd found even the three hours to Málaga bad enough.

They had arrived, Diana hopeful and excited, but had somehow checked into the wrong hotel. Someone there quickly alerted the hotel management to the true identity of one new guest. The Spanish press was duly tipped off. I *suppose* it is possible that an observant and enterprising chambermaid could have informed her bosses, having glimpsed Diana sans wig in her room. In any case, she was grounded. She called me despairingly, almost hysterical. She had spoken to Hewitt, she said, but there was no chance of a meeting and a 'drop' of her letters because the hotel was by now surrounded by paparazzi.

She was back in London in less than twenty-four hours, having managed to elude the press as she returned to the airport. She called me, in worsened distress, as soon as she left Heathrow. It would be charitable to describe this disaster as a dreadful chapter of accidents, but so much went wrong from the moment that she arrived in Spain that I wonder . . . After the publication of Hewitt's book, a great commercial success, Diana became convinced that the whole misadventure had been yet another attempt by him to wring money out of a relationship which she had once believed to have been concluded in a dignified, if sad, manner. She never would take receipt of her letters. They are now held at St James's Palace, passed on by a newspaper which had been offered them for publication.

Personal humiliation, bafflement, frustration and, above all, disappointment, plunged Diana into a withdrawn depression. She needed help after the Spanish fiasco, and care from me as, apart from Susie Kassem and perhaps Richard Kay, I was the only person she had confided in. The whole episode says much about her inexperience and trusting naivety where fierce romantic emotions were concerned. By the time she was ready to commit herself to a relationship again, she was looking not only for excitement, companionability and protection: she needed a man she could respect. It would be another year before she found him.

For despite what the lifted, angled gaze under the lashes of those extraordinary blue eyes might have suggested, Diana wasn't a flirt. That familiar image of her, with chin defiantly raised yet also tilted to one side and an expression both frank and blank, is much more deeply rooted in a little girl's longing for a father's attention and approval than in the adult, semi-sexual gazes and games of flirtation. Little girls, of course, flirt in their own expert and disingenuous way, often with their fathers, uncles and elder brothers' friends. But this is not the same adult teasing we generally understand as coquettishness. Even as a woman in her thirties Diana was too inexperienced to be skilled at this. Desperation could make her manipulative at times but her desires were for approval and acceptance. She was not seeking to use her undoubted power in a sexual way; she was testing it and stretching it to examine her own growth and find the limits of her own ground.

Diana committed herself totally to all of her few *romantic* attachments, beginning with Prince Charles and ending with the man closest to her heart before she started to enjoy life, all too briefly, with Dodi Fayed. There's little to be said about her soft spot for James Gilbey. Within that friendship, notable principally for the 'Squidgy' phone calls, Diana was merely playing dangerous telephone games. Having discovered the extent of the fragility of her marriage, she was exploring forbidden fields of possibility without much intention of seeing the implications of her actions through. Her most womanly emotions were not quite engaged.

With Oliver Hoare, however, Diana had behaved with an almost embarrassing naivety, believing that he could offer her more than he was willing or able to give. Such fault as there may have been lies with Diana rather than with Hoare, who probably only considered the lightest of flirtations with the world's most sought-after woman, as his restrained behaviour towards the end of their friendship confirms. This much is known: he was married, with family responsibilities to consider, and however entranced he may have been by Diana, however flattered by her attentions, he had other priorities.

By 1994 she had certainly become very attached to this society dealer in Middle Eastern art. Handsome, urbane and charming, he was perhaps terrifically flattered at first to find that he was of interest to her. Diana, hungry for the smallest affirmation of her worth, innocently mistook casual gallantry for other intentions. Her affair with James Hewitt was over, but with this new passion she seemed to be rescued from that reeling misery of rejection. Having been made to feel so valueless it was marvellous for Diana to be so apparently treasured. Thus began the frequent phone calls to him, each in their way begging for reassurance and acceptance. When Hoare's wife informed the police about the mystery caller who so often replaced the receiver when she answered the phone and the calls were traced to Kensington Palace, Diana denied any knowledge of them. A hapless schoolboy was briefly under suspicion of being the nuisance. Inevitably, this tale of telephone harassment and the Princess's alleged part in it reached the public.

In truth, Diana's pursuit of Hoare had been hopeless from the start. For some people—men and vampish women both—the thrill of the chase is the thing, and if their prey simply lies down in submission, their interest diminishes. But Diana was never a vamp: she was both too innocent and inexperienced, however drop-dead glamorous she could look. That she was no cold-hearted seductress is proved by the fact that, as I have said, even as late as 1995, just below the bodice seams or above the hemline of even her shortest skirts were the scratches and scabs of self-mutilation, long after the public believed that she had stopped attacking herself. She had no vamp's armoury to deal with her rejection by Oliver Hoare. I had suspected, from the shape and patterns of her scratches, that Diana's arsenal lay within the kitchen cupboard, the slender tines of a fork her preferred weapon . . .

Diana seldom discussed her friendship with Oliver Hoare with me, but like everyone else in the country, I had read about it. By then I knew her well enough to draw my own conclusions—namely, that she was perfectly capable of the sort of telephone tyranny that she had denied. I knew very well how reaching for the phone was a reflex for her, especially when excited or under stress, just as much as reaching for a cigarette or a drink is for others. Her protestations of innocence may have convinced some, but not me. My main concern was to help her never to make similar obsessive mistakes in the future. As I have said, her body still bore the marks of self-mutilation when I first met her, injuries that had been made essentially to call Hoare's attention to her residual need for him. That he would never have seen her wounds and so be roused to comfort her did not matter. She was beyond behaving logically. There hadn't even been a single defined moment of anger or disagreement between them for her to hang her upset on. She just couldn't understand why he didn't want her friendship. Diana, at that time, at least, was incapable of seeing that her humiliating recourse to self-mutilation would never rekindle the affection of, let alone kindle a non-existent affection in, a loved one. She could not see that the best she might hope for was pity, and that passion and pity seldom coexist. All this essentially confirmed to me that she wasn't yet ready to offer formal healing to others. She had a lot of self-sorting still to do.

When I did manage to speak to Diana about Oliver Hoare she agreed that her behaviour had been obsessive and self-destructive and we pretty much left it at that. She always made it very clear when she wanted to change the subject. But although the friendship with Hoare was over by the time I knew her well the emotional as well as physical wounds and scars were still raw and painful. She would have needed to know, even as he was retreating, that he was still there for her, that he might still be part of her life. I was never quite able to decide whether or not she had wanted him to leave his wife and family for her. To him Diana must have seemed like an insecure child, constantly wanting a kiss on the bruised knee or to have her fringe lovingly pushed out of her eyes. Any man would eventually find this stifling, even though Diana herself might not have thought that she was making heavy emotional demands. Often she would only be ringing him to touch base and pass on some little snippet of news about her day or enquire about his—just as she had once hoped to be able to communicate with her husband. Many people would be put off by this level of neediness, of course, but Diana, Princess of Wales, the world's icon and a famous beauty, simply could not understand why her phone calls were not returned.

By late 1995 she was calling me too, frequently. As already noted, she had, apart from anything else, a naive and dangerous belief that calls from mobile telephones could not be traced. If possible I'd interrupt whatever I was doing, personally or professionally, to take her calls, and would always ring her back the moment I could if she'd called while I was working. I'd try to offer encouragement and send strength down the phone to her if she seemed particularly distressed. I must admit, however, that sometimes I found her calls draining, however willing I was to take or return them. In the main I saw them as expressions of a rather charmingly childlike wish to share thoughts, responses and feelings, something which was entirely mutual where I was concerned. The worst time was at the height of her obsession with Hasnat Khan, when I had been asked—recommended by word of mouth, as usual—to cleanse a large house of seriously negative spirits. Although, or because, the bad energy in the house had been dispersed I was so utterly exhausted that I wasn't able to return all the messages about her worries she'd left on my answering machine. I thought she'd understood when one message simply began with a resigned 'You're probably out ghost-hopping . . .'

I'd told her several times that there was no point in pursuing a happily married man and that she had been misreading the signals. Without actually saying she was making a fool of herself, I told her that she was asking for trouble. Diana was not best pleased to hear this. By then I'd given her that dangerous little bit of learning about healing and human behaviour and she thought she knew better. But actually she wasn't ready to cope and even though I know that all human beings have to learn by their mistakes, I couldn't let her continue on this course of self-destruction without a few more sharp words of warning. Our friendship faltered a little after that row, but by the time she had come to realize for herself that the obsession with Oliver Hoare was pointless and unworthy of her we had patched it up. Diana was sometimes like that: a fierce quarrel could be forgotten and never referred to as the threads of friendship were re-woven without a word. Reconciliation invariably began with a phone call: 'Hi Simone, it's Diana—are you busy?'

After the row over Oliver Hoare in 1994 Diana had asked someone else to call me to cancel our next meeting. I thought this rather cowardly: I've never approved of people asking others to do their dirty work. Further-more, it suggested to me again that she truly wasn't ready to offer therapy herself if she was still relying on others to pick up the pieces when things weren't going too well for her. The next time I saw her I drew her aside and told her that I wasn't prepared to be treated like a servant or a tradesman. If she wanted to say something to me, I went on, she could do it herself, face to face.

Diana said nothing, but she understood what I meant. She looked at me steadily with those amazing eyes of hers and nodded. She called me again soon afterwards, for all the world as though nothing bad had happened. Our friendship resumed, bringing with it a saner and more sensible pace to Diana's learning about becoming a healer herself. Nothing more was said about the Oliver Hoare episode as we began talking and mending again.

There were to be plenty of disagreements between us ahead, but I was confident there would be no more failures to confront things properly. Diana seemed to have learned some very important lessons, not just those I had taught her about self-healing. These lessons continued informally through conversation, laughter and a general, broad exchange of ideas.

An inexperienced Diana, with raw and recent memories of a marriage that had failed, simply misread the runes about involvement with married men. It is difficult not to forgive her, given that *her* husband had shown that such infidelities can happen. She mistook charm and flattery for something altogether more serious. For a short while she had been joyful in her heady crush on Oliver Hoare, like a giddy schoolgirl. As she saw it, in dismal rejection lethally partnered with her own controlling tendencies, she was the most adored woman in the world and, by common consent, a legendary beauty. So why did Hoare prefer to remain with his family? Diana's experience of family life, both as a child and in early adulthood, had been severely and bitterly troubled, She'd somehow convinced herself that perhaps Oliver Hoare felt similarly, and that he would jump at the alternative offered. But there was never the suggestion of commitment from him. An insecure and baffled Diana was disabused of her girlish fantasies yet again, as she had been when the fairy tale of her marriage collapsed around her.

That arrested development and the crazed, adolescent way in which she dealt with her last relationship was not to be repeated, I thought. Surely through the pain she had learned lessons of self-control and restraint? But do we ever learn? Doesn't the next time we fall in love always seem like the first time?

But it would be untruthful to suggest that in the wake of the affair with James Hewitt, and her infatuation with Oliver Hoare, Diana found it impossible to enjoy diversions. She had many admirers and there were often rumours of non-existent affairs, some of them possibly fuelled by the press agents of men who would have liked to be publicly associated with her. Some of the men she was constrained to dance with at swanky charity balls might not have been flattered to hear what she said to me about them afterwards—belying the starry gaze she probably turned on them when she was briefly in their arms. (If someone wanted to convert a turn around the dance-floor into a serious smooch they would be disappointed as Diana expertly braced her hips and pelvis away from theirs whilst allowing one hand to rest lightly on their shoulder or arm.) After her divorce—and even during her separation—flowers, invitations and gifts would often arrive at Kensington Palace. There was an Italian count, an American billionaire and several other men. Naturally these attentions flattered Diana and at some level she enjoyed them. Sometimes she would spend a cheerful evening with one squire or another, but it was to be a long time before she was ready even to consider a whole-hearted relationship.

Moreover, although she was undoubtedly fond of Will Carling, the truth is that he was little more to her than any of her other therapists: she wanted to build up her muscle tone, and in time he became not merely her coach but a rare and treasured male friend to whom she found it easy to talk. That is the boringly simple reason why they used to meet in that Chelsea gym, and while there may have been a safe little flirtation going on in the first place it was quite insignificant compared to Diana's wish to demonstrate a physical strength and stature that matched her recently acquired mental resilience. She certainly owed something of her strengthened shoulders and toned physique to Carling's instruction, but not in the way that his wife imagined. I can only suppose that Julia Carling became alarmed when Diana—as the demanding and manipulative friend she could still sometimes be—had insisted that Will be on twenty-four-hour call. Julia could not have known that Diana did not find short men, however fit and muscular, sexually appealing. Carling is even shorter than Prince Charles, while Diana's preferred ideal was a man she could, literally, look up to.

Will Carling was simply one of a small number of devoted friends whom Diana relied upon at certain pivotal times in the last years of her life. And Julia Carling, even in misunderstanding her husband's almost chivalric attention towards the Princess, may have simply found a reason to stare into the face of a faltering marriage—her own. Speaking as his friend, Diana always maintained to me that Carling's marriage to Julia had been a mistake, as the couple had nothing in common. To his credit, Will Carling maintained his silence and his dignity when all the speculation about his relationship with the Princess was loudly and even lewdly aired. And he never attempted to take any credit for the physical repair that he had innocently helped her to achieve.

There was one wealthy American whom Diana had found sufficiently attractive to enjoy, early in 1995, a brief but intense liaison with. She was by no means certain, however, that he could be a long-term prospect, convinced though she was that one day she would re-marry. Her instincts were confirmed when she only half-jokingly asked him to endow a third-world hospital project to the tune of £21 million. After he baldly asked her exactly what return he could expect on his invest-ment her interest waned. There were a very few other dalliances: Diana wasn't quite as lonely as many people imagined. She also laughingly told me of a friend who cheekily asked her at one gala occasion if she was 'get-ting enough'—she retained too much respect and fond-ness for him to be offended. In the main she wanted to revert to the teenaged, innocent and unsexual role as 'one of the boys' she had played so well during her school holidays at Althorp—being there, being cheerful and learning from her older sisters as she watched them do the flirting with weekend visitors.

Diana's separation was to a considerable extent marked by her consultations with many seers and psy-chics. For years she maintained an absolute belief that if Camilla were no longer around she and Charles could make a fist of reconciliation. False hopes were offered, and Diana clutched at every straw. As late as 1994 she still clung to the hopes raised by a tabloid psychic, Betty Palko, who two years earlier had predicted that the Waleses would be reconciled. Diana never sought her ad-vice, but none the less took her unsolicited letters and readings quite seriously. She was hopeful and delighted and, seeing the optimism on her face, I felt wretched when she asked for my opinion and I could not truthfully offer her the assurances she still wanted so much to hear. Until the end she fussed and fretted about Charles's health as if they were still together and she still able lov-ingly to chide him.

But if Diana's hopes were easily raised, she also churned with worry all the time. The least important thing could upset her fragile balance. In 1996, after most of the tabloid newspapers published pictures of her with what appeared to be cellulite dimples on her upper thighs and buttocks, she became disproportionately distraught. I tried to convince her that the photographs could have been tampered with and that she had no such blemishes. But she was inconsolable and embarked upon a course of cellulite-reducing therapies and an even stricter than usual detoxing diet based around fruit and vegetable juices. 'I wish I had *your* cellulite,' I remarked to her, thinking about my own imperfect body. Incredibly, after a holiday in the West Indies she was especially upset about her figure, lamenting the fact that she didn't have a particularly well-defined waist. The sight of other, younger and—as she saw it—better bodies on the private beaches had genuinely distressed her, even though the women in question were professional models.

This extreme reaction says something about Diana's often self-destructive search for perfection. She had Will Carling to thank for her squared and muscular shoulders after she had been coached by him at the Chelsea gym where they were mistakenly supposed to have had romantic trysts. Conversely, perhaps, she could be oddly 'girlie'. Whilst I usually saw her without make-up and sometimes with her hair pulled back by an alice band, even when I went over to Kensington Palace for a private evening of gossip and TV Diana would occasionally have put on a lick of mascara and some lipstick if she'd had a meeting or some other previous engagement. Most days she would have had her hair immaculately styled after her return from working-out at the gym, even if she had only planned a simple day at home. She wanted to be feminine and tough all at once. Sometimes her friends didn't know where they were with her or which Diana they would encounter that day. This contributed, little by little, to the weakening or erosion of some of her friendships. For the Princess in her emotional limbo, this was tragic.

Many of her friends from school and the short period before her marriage were reticent about resuming contact now and Diana, terrified about further leaks, hesitated to reach out. After her separation the centre of her world—never solid—had dropped out. All she was left with was a core of regret and sadness and the bitter self-knowledge that she might not always be able to rely on the unconditional affection of old friends. Some of them felt that they had been thoughtlessly dropped when her life was being steered towards an unthinkably majestic future, a future with implications she had been far too young to understand, despite advice, when she accepted Charles's proposal of marriage in 1981. And now it seemed too late to pick up the threads of old friendships. For her part Diana—ever unwilling to accept that she could be in the wrong—was not prepared to build the bridges. Perhaps that is why she relied so much on someone like me who had no connection with her early life or the glossy pleasures of her current existence. I will say that when I first knew Diana I saw a strong contrast between the richness and commitment of her charity work and the emptiness—apart from her relationship with her sons—of her private life.

As well as the various friendships which were neglected after her marriage there were the trivial, imagined slights which could cause an increasingly paranoid

Diana to believe that people were against her. She had no problem with the mature, fatherly and respectful attentions of the likes of Sir Richard (now Lord) Attenborough or Lord Deedes (who would accompany her to the minefields of Angola and Bosnia in 1997). But some in her ever-diminishing circle were startled and hurt to be excised. Her former flatmate Carolyn Bartholomew, the very staunchest of her friends, was 'let go' even after a photographed hug had confirmed that Diana had approved of her contribution to Andrew Morton's *Diana, Her True Story*, published in 1992, and the book which, more than any other external factor, was to free the Princess from the nightmare of her loveless marriage. At various times such trusted friends as Susie Orbach, Lucia Flecha de Lima, Fergie and others all found themselves bafflingly and woundingly excluded.

Diana was not one to negotiate with during a row. Although this could be hurtful, as I can testify, I believe it demonstrated a lack of self-confidence and maturity rather than arrogance. Nor did she like to be outshone. Diana—who almost kept a mental record of her inches of press coverage—could spin into ludicrously competitive mode and terminate a friendship if she felt that association with her was bolstering another's vanity. Even now I find this aspect of her character strange since she had been so pathetically willing to accept—even call for—blame and responsibility for things going wrong in the past. I suppose it was simply the flexing of newly confident muscles, newly strong wings.

Loneliness, as much as anything, attracted Diana to her great range of healers and therapists. In much the same way bored and frustrated women all over the world trust and confide in their hairdressers in countless examples of a relationship which is both intimate and impersonal—the woman trusts the hairdresser to see her at her worst and will often, thus, confide. But in the end it is a business arrangement. This shortage of real unconditional friendships also helps to explain Diana's addictive telephone relationships with those few friends she *did* trust. Until late 1995 the physical side effects of her emotional pain were increasing, although she felt constrained to hide them in public. During the mid-1990s I observed an odd displacement aspect to her behaviour and feared that pressures might again be plunging her into severe distress. Diana became rather jealous if a friend—the more trusted the worse the effect—fell for someone. Quite simply, she became jealous of the friend in question's happiness if a new partner rendered them unable to give her the total commitment she sought, even demanded, and irrationally feared that she would lose them if they fell in love. Perhaps here she was subconsciously recalling the way *she* had neglected some of her old friends during the heady days of her engagement to Charles and the first few happy months of their marriage. And, of course, she would have remembered her own dismay when Frances, her mother, left her children to be with the man she loved.

Diana, paradoxically, had fallen prey to another syndrome now, one that I doubted I could help her escape from. At times she regarded herself as being so perfected and polished that only she could issue statements to the world about her state of mind. She came to believe that she needed her remaining friends less and less. While it was good to see her getting stronger, I still tried to help her keep her balance. We had a little bit of a spat, however, and that led to another brief rift.

She was also telling pointless lies more and more frequently, especially to the press. Usually these fibs could be explained by a very human and fundamentally understandable wish to spare others pain. 'Do I look OK?' 'Yes,' Diana would reply, 'You look terrific,' even if the person concerned looked below their best. Diana the pleaser was still in evidence in 1995. She would tailor the truth about this aspect or that of her life according to who she was speaking to and what she thought they wanted to hear. I suppose we all sometimes do this, but few of us compartmentalize as expertly as Diana could. Effusive flattery can put an intelligent person off as surely as unkindness. This was another facet of her self-destructiveness which I worried about.

She had begun telling me more of these silly little fibs. It might have been about what she had eaten, or she would stupidly deny that she'd seen certain therapists, as if I would have minded. When I questioned her about this untruthfulness Diana was contrite and promised to level with me in the future, and I believe she did try to. But she also retained a crazy conviction that, since she'd compartmentalized her life and had scattered about different versions of the same story, she would be safe and somehow protected. She never learned that it only took one person with a grudge, or one unguarded loose mouth, to unpick a thread in the stories she had woven. Even if good intentions had underpinned most of her small lies, the people whom she had deceived were often hurt. White lies are frequently the most dangerous ones . . .

At times in the past Diana had hoped to rely upon the support of her mother. Frances Shand Kydd had gone to live in Scotland, but she sometimes visited her youngest daughter. Diana *wanted* to be pleased to see her, not least because she was keen to talk through the unfinished business of her childhood. But these were troubled and uneasy encounters, especially after her mother was charged with a serious driving offence just as Diana's divorce was going through in 1996, a time when Diana felt she could do without any negative publicity about her family. Tensions also increased whenever Frances spoke to the press about her daughter without the latter's permission. All the resentments were rooted in the past, and I tried to urge Diana to understand a situation that she had been too young to appreciate at the time. Her older sisters had coped, I reminded her, and even if it was harder for her as the youngest daughter, she should try to forgive any hurt delivered in error or ignorance and to live in the light that she had been blessed with. Her mother, I said, must be well aware of the hurt she'd caused, and had suffered for it. To Diana, though, it was the ultimate grudge. Fond of her as I was, and as much as I admired her, there were times with her when I felt that I might as well have been bashing my head against a cotton-wool wall: she listened to advice, appeared to take it and then went her own way. I couldn't blame her for that—I could only hope that in time some of the things I'd said would sink in.

And then something happened which did more for Diana than a hundred therapies. She really fell in love. At last, and good and proper.

7

True Love

There was no mistaking Diana's state of euphoria. When anyone is on the emotional high of being newly in love the hormones reach the skin, the hair, the step, and above all the eyes. Early in the autumn of 1995 there was a lightness in Diana's voice, a skip in her stride and a sparkle in her glance that even the professional and dedicated Princess on duty could not have replicated. She was transformed. But she hugged her secret to herself for a little while as we played ourselves in, re-establishing trust.

Ironically, within the limitations of this complex new relationship she was suddenly able to behave more naturally and normally with the other people around her. She had focus again at last, and a new priority, even if her passion for Hasnat Khan forced her to embark upon a fresh series of dangerous deceits.

Our Kensington Palace evenings had restarted after that recent brief row, partly, I think, because I doubt if there was anyone else with whom she could discuss things like the advantages of a full leg wax over the bristly results of shaving or the slow agony of plucking the individual leg hairs out with tweezers. We were in agreement that the fast shriek of anticipated pain when the wax was ripped off was far preferable to the other slower options. She was even brave enough to endure the quick hell of having her underarm and bikini-line hair removed by wax every few weeks at Kensington Palace. We laughed about her memory of one almost sadistic beautician who had visited Diana at the palace to wax her legs. This woman's manner, she said, brought to mind that of an SS commandant, and she was not booked to return.

Diana was endearingly human about admitting to dealing with the occasional pimple. Like most women she found that an old, familiar and deeply disliked spot would break out on her chin or hairline at a particular time of the month, and we exchanged wisdoms about the effectiveness of mud masks as opposed to plasticized exfoliating ones to zap the zits. Sometimes we would talk about the lesser worry of shadows and bags under the eyes, but since I barely ever saw her affected by such minor flaws, unless a particularly troubled night had left a tiny shadow beneath her lower lashes, I did not feel that my recommendation of iced cucumber compresses would often be called for. She had a sunbed at home and, as everyone knows, liked to bask in the sun proper, but she was always very careful about taking care of her skin and rubbed salve and protective cream into it whenever she was out of doors. In any case, she preferred to walk, swim, play tennis or potter about, preferably with her boys, with a lovely heat enveloping her rather than to stretch out and bake.

Such 'girlie' chatter created the framework for a kind of informal confessional. It was within this newly affirmed atmosphere of relaxed intimacy that Diana first began to speak to me of her feelings for Hasnat Khan. I don't delude myself that the new confiding didn't have something to do with the fact that she had alienated so many of her society friends, but she also knew that she could trust me precisely *because* I had no connection with those few who remained. I often had dreams about Diana, and occasionally her mood would reflect the suggestions of the dream. Sometimes in the dreams I'd see her sitting alone and sobbing, sometimes she would be surrounded by people whom I sensed could harm her. It was refreshing to have a dream which convinced me that Diana was on the brink of great emotional happiness. When I told her I was sure she was going to become involved with a dark-skinned man and that he would be very important to her she laughed dismissively. She also laughed, albeit bitterly, when I assured her that one day she and Charles would become friends. But shortly after she secretly began to see Hasnat, even though she was yet to tell me about him, I had a strong sense that she was entering a very important new phase of her life and that it was connected with a man with whom she would become intensely emotionally involved. When I finally questioned her about this she confirmed that my instincts had been correct, but to be quite honest it would not have taken an Einstein to see that, during the autumn of 1995, she was on the brink of a great passion. It was a passion that would peak the following summer.

By the lift in her step, her general glow and a hundred other signs it would have been clear, even to those who did not know the Princess, that she was in that exquisite and simultaneously tormented state. This time, I thought, she was ready to handle things a little better than she had in the past. Having said that, however, one of the glories of the heightened, obsessed and infatuated state of being in love is that everyone forgets anything sensible they ever knew and treats the experience as if it were not only unique to them, but also unknown to anyone else in the world.

Hasnat Khan is a heart surgeon, then working at the Royal Brompton Hospital in Fulham under Professor Sir Magdi Yacoub. Diana had met him in September 1995 not through her friend Sir Magdi, as one might have supposed, but through her acupuncturist Oonagh Toffolo, whose husband was in the Brompton recovering from heart surgery. Thus it was through her caring and kindness for the partner of another therapist that Diana came to know this most important man. She had been visiting her friend's husband every day and had established something of a rapport with his surgeon. Somehow they seemed to meet on the steps of the hospital or find themselves standing in the lift as Diana was preparing to leave. She took all these coincidences as signs that something momentous and inevitable was waiting to happen. Certainly there was a strong chemistry that went far beyond Diana's undoubtedly genuine interest in the recovery of her friend's husband.

Few people who did not know the Princess well could have anticipated this turn of events. Hasnat Khan, a few years older than her and some inches taller, was a heavy smoker and enjoyed many of the 'wrong' foods. He carried more weight than he strictly should have done. At some stage during the late summer of 1995 Diana took her courage in her hands and told Hasnat that she would like to speak to him privately. Intense conversations at Kensington Palace started after that, Diana's collection of ashtrays spilling over with his cigarette butts. After August 1996 most of their meetings took place at the palace, with Hasnat leaving in the early hours before staff arrived if he had stayed the night with Diana. He had his own flat near by but it was easier and more private for them to meet at KP.

I have no doubt that Diana loved Hasnat. Nor do I have any doubt that she relished the mischief and sense of 'forbiddenness' that surrounded their affair. At KP once again only Paul Burrell was aware of this important new figure in the Princess's life, and for discretion's sake she would often borrow her butler's car for her meetings with Hasnat. In the mornings after seeing him she would seem as bright and rested as usual: no one needs much sleep when they are newly in love.

One can speculate that this was all something of an adventure for a girl who had been forced to grow up slightly before she was ready. But I think it was much more than that. Diana was seriously in love with Hasnat Khan, though not because he has 'oil-painting' good looks, because he doesn't, despite references to him in the tabloids as her 'dishy doctor'. What captivated her was Hasnat's wit, his intelligence and his dedication to work which she knew to be truly important. She was sometimes rendered inarticulate when she spoke to me of him, only able to describe him as 'a lovely man' or her 'Mr Wonderful', but her actions proved that she was utterly devoted to him. I thought that all this lent an interesting spin to the public opinion of a woman who was sometimes dismissed as being obsessed with appearances and the trappings of beauty. Diana, legally divorced by then, could do much as she pleased, but she was well aware that in this involvement she was risking criticism, even though it would be quite irrelevant to her divorce proceedings. The very fact that Hasnat's finest qualities were not necessarily apparent to the casual or thoughtless eye could generate gossip that she wished on neither of them.

Hasnat is the least materialistic of men and drove around—still does, for all that I know—in a clapped-out old car with a busted exhaust which had a tendency to backfire. Diana did *not* enjoy her very occasional drives with him in it, not least because she feared that routine police attention could blow their cover. She was all for buying him a new car but I advised against this, worried that she might already be in danger of being overly possessive and stifling in her affection for him.

I often spoke to or saw Diana just before she was due to meet Hasnat, and her excitement was palpable. If she had time she would take special care with her make-up and outfit, but if she received an urgent call from him on her mobile she would fly out of the palace within minutes. No time then to fix her face, hair or clothes. Only his calls, in my observation, could make Diana foreshorten any telephone conversation she might be taking on another line. She had butterflies in her stomach before any meeting and lost her appetite, like any other woman in love. She veered between heights of soaring joy and depths of depressed insecurity. In fact, she was behaving quite normally except in the tactful discretion she exercised in protecting Hasnat's privacy—something that was perhaps even more important to him than it was to her.

He might have suggested a meeting in a pub near his hospital or at a simple fish-and-chip restaurant. Diana would scribble down directions and dash, careful none the less to drive by a circuitous route in order to give possible watchers the slip, even if her destination was very close. She definitely didn't share his liking for Southern fried chicken or large amounts of lager; in fact, she sometimes remarked that Hasnat would need his own heart surgery before long, but she loved his company and would sometimes daydream with me about the kind of life they might make together. I suspect that she thought she could chivvy him out of his bad habits, and I remember how she laughed when I remarked that I couldn't quite see the appeal of fish suppers or smoky pubs. But then, I wasn't the one whose emotions had been fully engaged at last.

Hasnat was passionate about modern jazz and he aroused in Diana her own appreciation of it. They often went to darkened clubs in Soho or Camden Town together, late at night. In one of her wigs and suitable make-up she was quite unrecognizable. This, coupled with the fact that she would have chosen very anonymous casual clothes and was escorted by a slightly overweight Asian man, made these secret outings with Hasnat perfectly safe as well as thrilling for her. She was hiding in plain sight. Queueing was a novelty to her, almost an adventure—once she phoned me excitedly to say that they had been waiting in line for an hour to get into Ronnie Scott's, Hasnat having gone to the desk to find out how much longer they would have to wait. I never ceased to be flabbergasted by Diana's pleasure in such 'thrills' and just told her I queued in Tesco and Marks & Spencer every day, so couldn't see the charm of them.

All this was rather like an extension of the mantle of anonymity she had become able to assume when she walked with me and a small group of dowdy and casually dressed friends over Hampstead Heath. But I was pleased to see her so very happy.

She was so impatient to have Hasnat's undivided attention that if he used the Kensington Palace telephones to speak to his family or friends in Pakistan for more than ten minutes Diana would turn her music up or dance before him to distract his attention. Sometimes she'd call me to tell me what was happening and I could tell she was speaking with the phone crooked under her chin as she played her piano. But there were dangers for Diana within this euphoric and possessive state. She took to calling Hasnat at inconvenient times for him, and was often upset if he was in the operating theatre and couldn't talk to her. I had gathered that he was not the most emotionally demonstrative or articulate man at the best of times, so at moments like these Diana would ring me, depressed and jittery in case she was losing him. Over and over again she repeated how much she cared for him. She had given him simple meals at Kensington Palace and fantasized about a life where they could live together in some semblance of normal domesticity, speculating about the possibility of their making a real life together. She wanted to be just plain 'Mrs' and had the fanciful idea of living in Australia, where Hasnat had worked for a time, or America. She even had people looking for houses for them, believing that their romance could flourish if Hasnat could get out from beneath the shadow of Sir Magdi Yacoub, the heart surgeon who was training him. She went as far as getting in touch with her friend Christian Barnard, the famous South African surgeon, with the idea that she and Hasnat might move to South Africa. She was now focusing her attentions on that country and on America, having decided, after spending just two or three days in Sydney during an official visit to Australia, that she couldn't live there.

With this in mind, she introduced her boys to Hasnat

some months after they had become close. Although both her sons were predictably polite to him, William took a particularly mature attitude, telling her that the relationship was OK by him 'if it makes you happy, Mummy'. But Hasnat was uneasy. As Diana told me, he wasn't ready to become stepfather to two very self-possessed adolescents, and especially not to William, the heir to the throne. She, however, driven by her desire to have a little girl, remained optimistic that things could work out. Diana may indeed have been indulging in wishful thinking. Both before and after her death Hasnat, while speaking of the Princess with the warmest respect and affection, has said that no such plans had been made.

She wanted to know all about Hasnat, to delve into every aspect of his life. When two of his oldest friends from his village in Pakistan arrived in Britain with a barely thought-out business proposal Diana arranged a meeting for them with Richard Branson. In the event this was not a success as 'Tweedledum and Tweedledee', as Diana referred to them, one being fat and the other very skinny (she had misremembered her Lewis Carroll here, as both Tweedles are rotund in *Alice in Wonderland*), had not done their homework. In such ways Diana wanted to please Hasnat; moreover, she hoped that her interest in his work could attract funding for the British Heart Foundation. She was certainly willing to commit herself publicly to this. But in her eagerness to please and to have shared concerns with him she may well have been stifling a delicate flame . . .

Driven at least in part by her obsession with the importance of family life, Diana visited some of Hasnat's relations in Stratford-upon-Avon, where she and he had spent long evenings in restaurants. She stayed with these members of his family several times, helped to prepare meals and to clear up afterwards, thrilled to be thus welcomed by the family, and taking the fact that Hasnat didn't always drive up with her as evidence of relaxed acceptance, just as if she was one of the family. In the spring before her death Diana had promised Jane, the wife of Hasnat's brother Omar, the gift of a pram for the baby she was expecting. Yet even in meeting members of his family there were dangers lurking. In 1996 and early 1997, while ostensibly on a trip to visit her friend Jemima, formerly Goldsmith, but by then married to Imran Khan, and somewhat to Hasnat's alarm, Diana had also visited members of his family in Pakistan. This journey may have been her undoing. Giving her official driver the slip, Diana visited Hasnat's family home in Lahore. So enthusiastic were some relatives there about this 'private' visit that newspaper articles appeared about an 'eastern romance', avowing that the Princess was regarded as a daughter of the house. However distorted some of these stories may have been, the private aspect of Diana's relationship with Hasnat was nearly over. And so, effectively, was any romance.

Perhaps Hasnat had already become wearied by those calls on his bleeper at inappropriate times. Certainly, however much he may have loved Diana, he was unready to assume all the baggage that marriage to her would entail. With agonizing irony she, who admired his work and purpose so much, was forced to see his point. After over eighteen months things between them were cooling.

I believe that Diana was fatally mistaken when she made the trip to Pakistan without telling Hasnat of her plans. She wanted to meet his family, although her public pretext was to visit Jemima Khan and to help with the raising of funds for a children's cancer hospital with which Imran Khan was involved. The fact that she simply, if naively, wanted to learn more about Hasnat by meeting other people close to him cut no ice. He knew her well enough to know that she was almost obsessional about families and longed to be embraced by them—whether it was, for instance, the Goldsmiths, or his own—but his own need for privacy was paramount and he was alarmed. As a result, when news of the relationship reached the British press Hasnat assumed that Diana had leaked it and was further concerned.

Late one spring evening in 1997, having been called to Kensington Palace, the sight of a distraught Diana with swollen panda eyes and mascara-streaked cheeks made my heart weep with her. I could empathize so well with her misery and, far from being wearied by the summons, I was just glad that I could be there for her. She was both mortified and panic-stricken because she felt that Hasnat was withdrawing from her. Despite a strong sense of injustice and wounded pride, she believed it somehow to be her fault. Journalists from all over the world had tracked him down and, in his alarm, Hasnat had told her that he wanted to step away. In fact, the 'culprit' and source of some of the newspaper gossip was probably an elderly and impoverished relation of Hasnat's. While Diana didn't mind that at all, she felt guilty that her public persona should be affecting a 'normal' relationship.

Whatever the background to this crisis, Diana blamed herself. Perhaps she saw his behaviour as another betrayal, except that this time a man she cared for had chosen to stand loyal to, indeed to absolve, a member of his own family rather than brace himself and stand beside Diana to face the world. Her tears that evening therefore derived from a conflicting mixture of self-directed guilt, frustrated disinclination to carry the blame after all her efforts to respect Hasnat's need for privacy, and sheer, angry misery about the prospect of losing the man she loved.

In a way, all Diana's double bluffs and little leaks of misinformation to the press were coming home to roost since, ironically, this crisis had been exacerbated by her feeding inaccurate information to one of the few journalists she could truly trust—Richard Kay.

In November 1996, when both Diana and Richard were in Australia, and after a splash by the *Sunday Mirror* about her romance with Hasnat, she gave Richard the 'ammo' for a story which categorically refuted any idea that she was involved with the heart surgeon. Published in the *Daily Mail* on 4 November, the piece trumpeted: 'Princess Diana succinctly described a report that she was in love with a doctor as "b******t"', before going on to quote 'one of her aides' who, having denounced the *Sunday Mirror*'s report as 'nonsense', said: 'It is no secret the two are friends, but in an entirely professional way. Mr Khan is one of many doctors the Princess knows at the Brompton and Harefield hospitals in London. That is all there is to it.' Richard's article also said that Diana was deeply upset at the allegation, as well as concerned about her sons' possible reaction to it, although it added that she had laughed with friends about the very idea.

This last inference may have upset Hasnat deeply, causing Diana further anguish since the lines she had fed to Richard had been issued to *protect* Hasnat and the privacy she knew he guarded so assiduously. In desperation she tried to redress the balance by feeding a balancing story to another newspaper. But it was too late. Hasnat had experienced the glare of the publicity that came with the territory if someone was even rumoured to be involved with the Princess, and he did not like it.

When, miserably frustrated and upset, Diana spoke to me of all this I asked why she didn't just tell Richard the truth? Maybe even now he could set things straight. Her reply was sad, and made me even sadder. How, she asked, could she start telling the truth *now* when to do so would expose all the lies of the past? Here, then, was another instance of Diana finding it hard ever to admit to being in the wrong. A few days before the anniversary of her death, Hasnat Khan spoke briefly to the *Daily Express* and refused to deny or confirm that his relationship with the Princess had been a physical one. The statement, cautious as it is, is in marked contrast to his earlier emphatic dismissals of any such possibility.

As another example of her 'playing' of the press, when Diana heard that Clive Goodman of the *News of the World* was writing an exposé of Hasnat, she asked me to call the journalist and tell him that she was still seeing Oliver Hoare.

She needed my support again. I knew that in the short term I had helped her to find enough strength to deal with the crisis, but I also knew that she remained heartsick from this latest abandonment, and that she would have to cope with things in her own way. Diana, however, chose to take an age-old but nevertheless risky course. History and literature are littered with examples of women who mistakenly believe that by inspiring jealousy they will revive and regain a weakening love . . .

Once again Diana was reeling with rejection. But she *was* stronger now, and able to show Hasnat, Charles and the world that she was ready to have some fun, and that she was not prepared to do so in secret or in disguise. Not long afterwards, in July, she began her short and exhaustively reported summer friendship with Dodi Fayed. She had not allowed the press to glimpse her outings with earlier admirers for whom she felt only passing affection and with whom she may have indulged in the recently learned skills of innocent flirting. But now she welcomed the media. Diana may have had other items on her agenda, but in the meantime this was as serious as flirtation gets.

In this last liaison Diana—I think for the first and only time—indulged in a little emotional manipulation where romance was concerned. It was to the world, not merely to her former husband, that she wanted to show that she was alive again and ready to be complete as a woman during those fourteen or so long-overdue indulgent days that she spent with Dodi. But she was also hoping to send messages to a very private individual.

We all know that the jolt of love at first sight can bring with it intense feelings and an irrationally strong belief that the soul has met its missing twin. But I believe it to be nonsense to imagine that someone as canny as Diana—at least, in some ways—was prepared to commit herself to that new relationship with Dodi quite so quickly. She was in the bloom of womanhood and health and could take her time. She and Dodi had known each other slightly for years before things between them appeared to blossom into something deeper. But still she was in no rush: she had her boys to consider, as she had also to consider the question of religious faith in the context of marriage to a Muslim, as well as her own place in the hearts of the British.

No—I think that finally she felt sufficiently relaxed and free enough to brave a public fling in a way that had never been open to her, or even possible, before. And at last she could allow herself to be a little reckless, if not exactly naughty. All those years ago the schoolgirl had been very, *very* good, and had won prizes for being kind to others. Thereafter she had been constrained to be dutiful, nice, wifely, decorative and quiet during her marriage. Afterwards came the not entirely welcome type-casting as a saintly, tragic victim. There was some truth in each of these refractions from Diana's prism—but in her relationship with Dodi Fayed she was displaying a new facet. In some ways a late developer, she had grown up and was simply having some adult fun. It made a change, too, for her to be with someone who actually encouraged publicity and who was happy to provide her with expensive toys to play with.

Most importantly of all, however, Diana was still in love with Hasnat Khan. I believe that on her secret agenda was the idea of reawakening the feelings of the man she had adored for the past two years. Her attachment to him was very different from either of her previous two post-marriage romantic obsessions, and different, too, from the current joyous fling with Dodi Fayed.

Certainly she was openly happy with Dodi, deliriously enjoying some freedom in sunny places, forgetting both the cloak and the dagger for once. Her heart may have cracked and ached again, but this time she was going to deal with the pain in a different way. Diana, of all women, was due that passing pleasure, but I don't think she was in love with Dodi. Having suffered more than enough at the hands of cool, emotionally retentive Englishmen, she was attracted to the honest, emotional and optimistic character of Asian and Latin men. Being with Dodi was a logical and enjoyable diversion from her troubled relationship with Hasnat—no more and no less than that.

Dodi's father, Mohamed al-Fayed, fanned the flames of rumour during his son's fatal friendship with Diana, and has suggested that his son and the Princess had been on the brink of announcing their engagement when they were killed. I know that I am not alone in thinking that this is little more than wishful speculation, separate from his grief at the death of a beloved son. Dodi and Diana had enjoyed a friendly but passing acquaintanceship in the past. She knew his father well enough to have prevailed upon Fayed, the Christmas before she died, to help her out over that KP staff lunch, but she had no deep and long-standing bonds with his family. As for the famous 'engagement' ring—I have my doubts about this. Diana was always like a child about presents, excitedly telling any friend she spoke to about a recent gift. She mentioned this ring neither to her sisters nor to Richard Kay, all of whom spoke to her in the hours before she died. We all certainly saw pictures of a spectacular diamond ring, heavy with gold as well as stones and not obviously reflecting Diana's taste. It may simply have been a present—Dodi was a rich and generous man, after all, and that, I think, is the end of it.

Above all, her boys would have known if Diana had been considering marriage to Dodi Fayed, just as they had been tentatively shown that their mother was serious about Hasnat. The fact that Dodi laid on discos and other entertainments for them during that summer in the Mediterranean reflected his lavish and generous style, not their mother's long-term intentions.

I'm convinced that Diana's subtext, her aim in this affair with Dodi Fayed, was to taunt Hasnat Khan, inspire his jealousy and make him reconsider things. Yet in a cooler part of her heart and brain she would have known that the very aspects of Hasnat that she loved most—his commitment to his work and his need for a normal existence—would render partnership with or marriage to her difficult, if not impossible.

'Can you really imagine being plain old Mrs Khan?' I'd asked her countless times. She would smile and say, yes, she could, but then her face would cloud. In her heart Diana knew that if she married again it would have to be to a figure very eminent in the Establishment—although not necessarily the British Establishment—and a very rich figure at that. And when I reminded her that she was the mother of the future King of Great Britain, Diana would look up, shrug, and say 'Why don't you let me dream a bit more?'

Within this new trap she was sad, partly because she knew she had, for once and at last, to take some personal responsibility for her place in that cage. The hedonistic summer distraction with Dodi Fayed was an escape, however brightly she smiled for the paparazzi that August. And I believe that Diana would have had some sadness in her heart on the day she died, however dazzling that last smile was.

Hasnat Khan was on holiday when Diana was killed. He arrived home to find, among the accumulated post waiting for him, a birthday card from the Princess—and an invitation to her funeral. On 6 September 1997, he was an inconspicuous and quietly devastated presence in Westminster Abbey, his pass arranged by Paul Burrell. He had always shunned the scrutiny of the public gaze, and has largely evaded it since Diana's death, just as quietly as he slipped into her life during the last, glowing, two years of it.

8

Diana in Disguise

What do you think?'

Someone from her office had led me upstairs and as I entered her sitting room Diana twirled in front of me. I was silenced. It was the first time I had seen her in the long dark brown wig.

She was recognizable because she hadn't adapted her make-up and was dressed in a familiar formal suit in readiness for an engagement later on. But Diana certainly looked *different*. She was having a trial run with this dramatic new wig, having already briefly fooled the boys in it, but she wasn't yet quite ready to wear it in public. It had been bought, discreetly, in Selfridges, the vast and yet somehow anonymous department store in Oxford Street. Later Sam McKnight, who made nearly all Diana's other wigs, would need to cut and style it a bit more before she was completely satisfied. The wigs Sam created for the Princess really were masterpieces which moved and flopped and settled and sprang like real hair—unlike most wigs, even expensive ones. Other hairdressers have pointed out that wigs, even expertly made ones, usually tend to be too thick to replicate the swing of natural hair, as though the maker has tried to forestall purchasers' determination to get their money's worth. So even the best ones need to be thinned, trimmed, shaped and tended just as carefully as a real head of hair, and with Sam McKnight Diana's disguises were in first-class hands.

She had quite a collection, built up after she first began to go out in public with Hasnat. As well as the long dark brown one there was a mid-length, mid-brown version with blond highlights, a shortish, bubble-cut mid-blond one, and at least two others. I wouldn't say that this wide variety had been chosen to reflect differing moods, however: her thinking was much more practical than that. For Diana the wigs were part of a means of achieving privacy and thus freedom, so it made sense to ensure that no particular hairstyle or look became so familiar as its wearer exited Kensington Palace that questions would be asked and the driver followed. For the same reasons Diana sometimes borrowed Paul Burrell's car or a Rover from the KP garage, rather than drive her own BMW.

Although she had not, for years, had any desire to grow her own hair below her ears, Diana particularly liked her longer, darker wigs for the simple anonymity which they bestowed. She sometimes wore them with spectacles specially fitted with clear glass lenses. Her make-up would always be influenced by the wig she had chosen on any given day. With the use of brownish, russet and olive tones in her eyeshading, lipsticks and foundation, rather than the blues and pinks that went so well with her fair hair and natural colouring, she could radically change her appearance. On those days the rather sweetly old-fashioned device she employed to give her cheeks a natural blush—that of pinching them with her fingertips—would be neglected. Only when she was wearing one of her wigs would Diana apply a slash of scarlet or deepest crimson to her lips, or lay darker cosmetic shadows beneath her cheekbones. Her excitement in these experiments was rather like that of a little girl playing at her mother's dressing table or rummaging through the dressing-up box.

It's also possible that Diana, not quite a natural blonde, was perversely reacting against the negative typecasting that being fair-haired can sometimes provoke. Blondeness can be a short-cut cliché, suggesting to some people a dim and blowsy sensuality and, to others, a glacial aloofness. Diana wanted to inspire neither response: she wasn't a peroxide bombshell nor yet some Nordic ice queen. However, she had to take some personal responsibility for the golden tresses that princesses of fairy tale and myth are so often blessed with. Her blondeness, as any brief glance at fair-to-mousy childhood photographs of her will confirm, was expertly assisted. Already slightly disguised, then, the collection of wigs was therefore a kind of complicated double bluff.

I always thought it was odd, if quite funny, that despite wearing her wigs with confidence and ease, Diana would never admit to having her fair hair 'helped'. She once almost chided me for admitting quite breezily that my hairdresser had put a colour rinse on my hair, and said she couldn't understand why I was so open about it. Ladies, she averred, never came clean about that sort of thing. This reminded me of the old adage that horses sweat, gentlemen perspire but ladies simply glow . . . I suppose that partly explains why she was so unnecessarily secretive about her own highlights; she was loath to acknowledge—even to friends—that something wasn't natural, or somehow all her own work. I think that something of the same attitude at times underpinned her work for charities. Of *course* her office would brief her before an engagement and distil and simplify important information for her, but Diana doggedly tried to read and understand many of the more complex background books and documents, not only as a genuine attempt to contribute, but also so that no one could accuse her of taking short cuts.

It was observed that the stronger or more self-assertive Diana became over the years after her marriage first showed signs of collapsing, the higher would be her heels, as if symbolizing a determination not to be crushed. However, when she went out incognito she tended to dress down, wearing flat shoes and her most inconspicuous, casual high-street-store clothes, because the main point of these excursions—other than seeing Hasnat, of course—was to allow her a glimpse of freedom and anonymity. Apart from the ever-faithful Paul Burrell, me, her sons, Hasnat Khan, and Susie Kassem during the fateful flight to Spain when Diana wore the dark blond bubble-cut wig, none of her friends saw her like this or had any inkling of her little habit of going out in disguise. Being kitted up in this way contributed to the thrill of being with Hasnat, certainly, and enabled them to eat and drink in public and in peace and go to clubs together as an ordinary couple. But even without that relationship I think Diana would have needed this means of escape sometimes.

Her sons knew all about Diana's little forays in disguise. Children understand the importance of what they call 'dressing up' and William and Harry thoroughly approved of their mother's occasional makeovers. They thought it was rather funny, and were mature enough to realize that she needed a private life as well as a public one, that sometimes she simply wanted to stop being the Princess of Wales for a little while and walk down a street, browse in a shop or sit in a park, without having to rely on the public's tact and sensitivity to observe her wish for privacy and leave her alone.

Diana told me that once she had arranged to meet someone in the concourse of a tube station in London and as she waited she noticed two young men staring at her. At first she feared that she might have been recognized, but when she overheard one say to the other that he really liked the look of the woman 'over there', and then mutter audibly that he wouldn't mind 'giving her one', she realized she was safe. She told me about all of these little outings and we laughed about this incident afterwards, wondering how the lads would have reacted if she had whipped off her wig and offered to discuss the proposition.

One day I arrived at Kensington Palace to find Diana experimenting with blue nail polish. She'd just painted the nail of one little finger and we both admired the colour, but she wouldn't paint them all. She was, after all, still the Princess of Wales. She rolled her eyes upwards and laughed when I suggested that she try a temporary electric-blue streak in her hair. I thought it would have looked marvellous with her natural colouring, but this idea, too, she smilingly dismissed. I find it interesting and, again, paradoxical that she was willing to take the dramatic step of adopting full disguise but not quite ready to flaunt position and protocol with a single blue streak when she was being the 'real' Diana.

Whereas she might tip off the media if she was making a 'private' visit to someone whose charitable cause she wanted to help, obviously she never alerted the press about these most secret of her activities, not least because her disguises were partly designed to fool journalists and photographers. However gracefully she dealt with them, Diana actually hated crowds and flashbulbs. She used to speak to me of 'the vultures', people who wanted to 'pick away at her, piece by piece'. It was therefore with a mixture of good humour and relief to be back home at KP that she pored over pictures of her being crowded by fans and paparazzi in Italy. 'Spot the Diana,' she said to me as she pointed to the top of her head within the crush in one picture. But while she could be mildly amused then, she had hated the whole business at the time.

There had been other 'incognito' episodes she had hated, too. One of her few post-marriage experiences of flying tourist class was when she went to Spain wearing her bubble-cut wig. Given the distressing nature of her mission, the uncomfortable flight conditions and the dehydration that can afflict even those travelling in Club Class, I'm not surprised that she flew with her own head of hair freely exposed ever afterwards. Actresses remark upon the relief from itching—amongst other things— that they feel when peeling off a wig after a stage performance in normal air conditions. For Diana, wearing a wig during that tense flight must have been little short of torture.

In fact, I had helped her to develop a different form of subterfuge and disguise for occasions when wigs and uncharacteristic clothes weren't possible—when, for instance, she wanted a short space of strengthening anonymity before heading off directly to some engagement at which she had to be 110 per cent Princess of Wales. Essentially, I coached Diana in the art of pretending to be someone who bore a strong passing resemblance to the Princess.

Quite a few women could, with a little artifice, look slightly like her and often copied her style. A number of them have even made careers out of the resemblance, ensuring that their wardrobes, make-up and hairstyle mirrored whatever phase Diana was in at the time. An effective disguise doesn't depend upon theatrical props like wigs or fancy dress: it can be in the mind if the person is determined to preserve anonymity and willing to take the risk of 'hiding' in plain sight. The best place to hide a pebble is on the beach . . . How often have you seen someone in the street, in a shop or on the train who reminded you of some celebrity? The chances are that once or twice the person you saw was indeed the famous star you vaguely thought they resembled. But because they were in an unlikely place, perhaps doing something as mundane as taking money from a cashpoint or hailing a cab, you assumed that you were mistaken: *That luminary could never inhabit the same mundane streets as you, could they? Or be wearing a coat similar to the one you bought last year in John Lewis? That star would never have untidy hair or be doing something just as normal as you that day, surely?* So you shrug and think no more about it.

In the spring of 1996 Diana and I formed a pleasant habit of meeting for lunch at a friend's house in Hampstead, she having driven there and parked in a quiet side street. When it was fine enough and after eating our lunch we'd sit on the terrace that overlooked the Heath, and afterwards we'd walk over the lovely muddy tracks and breathe that clean air provided by old trees which help to make the city's parks, as they have been described, 'the lungs of London'. We were a thoroughly nondescript group, bundled in ordinary warm clothes and boots if the weather looked threatening and attracting no attention whatsoever from the other strollers out with their dogs or kids. Now and again Diana would inspire a double-take but there was never any intrusion, even on a day when a later arrangement had forced her to dress more formally than usual.

I'm convinced that the way in which we were ignored during those walks cannot be entirely credited to the natural reticence and good manners of the people of Hampstead, but stemmed largely from the fact that no one expected to see Diana there—she became effectively invisible amidst a small group of nondescript walkers. On other days, when Diana and I had acupuncture appointments in Camden Town, just down the hill from Hampstead, she and I would look in shop windows as we strolled about before or after our treatments. Diana might admire a dress or blouse in a shop-window display but she would never go inside to try anything on, although she may have made a mental note to contact the shop later. If, however, she saw some pretty little thing—a vase, brooch or scarf that she felt might be perfect for some friend's birthday—she'd step into the shop and buy it. She always paid by credit card but I have no idea what she signed as. I think it was probably Diana Wales, but it could have been as Diana Spencer or Frances Spencer. Who knows? I'm certainly not sure—it's just not the sort of thing you stop to wonder about when you're out shopping with a friend.

In Camden we'd sometimes stop for coffee and occasionally a croissant in one of the cafés. So confident had Diana become as an impersonator of herself that if someone there gave her a wide-eyed and puzzled stare she would smile and wave at them, as if daring them to challenge her. I could tell how important these small escapes were for her when her face fell and she glanced at her watch, knowing it was time to return to Kensington Palace or to make an official appearance somewhere else. Then, like Cinderella in reverse, we would have to leave the quiet but pleasant normality and head back towards the place where she'd left her car.

Quite often if she was out on one of these jaunts and not particularly dressed-up or glamorized, Diana would stop to speak to a tramp or down-and-out, realizing that they, of all people, would be unlikely to recognize her, especially if they were elderly or unusually befuddled. She would find a shop and buy some food for them, and perhaps hand over enough change for a hot drink as well, before scribbling down for them the addresses of nearby shelters for the homeless (she had visited so many of these that she retained details in her head). And then she would be gone, pleased to have been able to help a little but frustrated not only because she could not do more, but also because the social injustice existed in the first place. She mentioned doing this in 1994 when, after lunch with friends in Knightsbridge, she had noticed an elderly vagrant on a bench as she headed home. She got in her car and went to a pizza restaurant, bought the old man some food, gave him some advice and a little money and then drove back to Kensington Palace. It was to become something of a habit.

It's hard for the rest of us to imagine how desperately Diana missed the simple freedoms which most of us take for granted, and to realize how necessary for her were those snatched hours when she could pretend to be, not exactly another person, but the person she might have remained if she hadn't married into the royal family. There were times for Diana when the idea of a good look around Marks & Spencer, a browse in a gallery, a coffee at a table outside a street café and a dawdle home were much more appealing than five-star this, first-class that and all the other trappings by which she was caged.

Sometimes at night, particularly if she couldn't sleep, Diana would clear out a cupboard and stuff black plastic bin liners with clothes she no longer liked or wore. These would be her everyday things rather than the formal designer outfits which she felt it proper to preserve almost as museum pieces. Those nights she would get in her car and drive alone round London, stopping outside charity shops where she would leave the bags in the doorway. It's a startling and sobering thought to consider that any one of us—or more probably, anyone forced by necessity to rely on charity shops for clothing for themselves and their family—might have picked up one of the Princess's T-shirts or jerseys, a pair of leggings or some shoes, without knowing who had worn them last. She gave me a lot of the outsized T-shirts she sometimes wore to sleep in, if she had tired of the colour or design.

Secret nocturnal visits to shelters for the homeless comprised another important aspect of Diana's most personal life. She would drive herself to places which she knew to be open, appearing unannounced. If there had been food to bring from Kensington Palace I'm sure she would have taken it with her, but since there would only have been some wilting salad in her own kitchen, taking food with her wasn't an option.

But she did bring boundless caring and empathy to the disadvantaged. She had particular concern for people who had lost touch with or been rejected by their families, and it was not in vanity that she knew she could restore *something* to them. Diana was aware of her gifts and power, and she was not going to waste them. This sort of unglamorous, unpublicized work in uncomfortable surroundings can hardly have been pleasant for her. But she knew she was privileged, and wanted to offer what she could—her presence, her time and her concern; moreover, it would have been against her nature to restrict such visits for fear of being found out and labelled a lady bountiful. Where that sort of thing was concerned, Diana didn't care what other people thought or what incorrect constructions they put on her motives.

When she had first become convinced of her abilities as a healer, Diana had offered to go and work with Mother Teresa among the poor of Calcutta. Her request was gently but firmly rejected. The famous missionary felt that at that stage the Princess was still too needy to work effectively, the suggestion being that she was motivated as much by a wish for further therapy of her own as she was driven by a desire to work selflessly for others. I was not surprised that Mother Teresa took this view, although I was saddened to see Diana so dejected by it. By a curious irony, the tiny Albanian-born missionary and the tall and exquisite princess died within a week of each other. In fact, Mother Teresa did later revise her opinion of Diana. Things could have been so different by now.

In a strange way, I think that the tiaraed and otherwise dazzlingly bejewelled Princess, designer-dressed way beyond the nines, was just as much in disguise as she was when she ventured out alone in very plain clothes. Everyone knows that Diana loved beautiful clothes, and it would be foolish to suggest that she didn't relish the opportunities of wearing them. But those wonderful outfits and the image she was obliged to project when she wore them had come to represent a person from whom she felt increasingly and oddly detached. She was on stage when she wore those magnificent outfits and gowns, and her performance was stunning. But, increasingly, it was just that—an act. Andrew Morton has told us that as early as 1994, in conversation with the Oscar-winning movie star Jeremy Irons, Diana remarked that she had given up acting.

But if the manner in which she wore clothes—formal or casual—was one thing, what she wore beneath them was quite another. I have to admit to being shocked at first when I realized that Diana often set off for some grand or otherwise important public or social occasion without wearing any panties. Or on private visits, come to that: the occasion might as easily have been a visit to her acupuncturist as an appearance at Ascot.

If her dress was sheath-like, if her trousers were expertly tailored, and even if her skirt was simply a clingy or bias-cut mini, Diana wanted to avoid the dreaded VPL—'visible panty line'. In explanation she implied that it insulted the garment, and indeed the designer, if the lines of the skirt or trousers were flawed by the signs of underwear. I could see her point about that—after all, most of her formal dresses had bust support built into them so that she never had to worry about bra straps showing—but somehow the idea of going out without one's panties seemed more extreme. Perhaps because millions of women of my generation were finger-wagged by their mothers into the idea that immaculate underwear was an everyday essential—just in case disaster struck . . .

Diana had no such bourgeois worries and would smooth the skirt or trousers over her hips, happy to look over her shoulder and check in the mirror that no offending lines were visible. She would always wear sheer, cotton-gusseted tights, however, so she was not actually naked under those outfits, however cheekily she may have briefly flashed her thighs as she climbed out of her official car or glided across a lawn towards an evening gallery opening. I think there was something rather girlishly mischievous about this—something beyond Diana's wish to show her clothes to their best advantage. That panty-less state was her secret, and thus another form of disguise.

Diana's entirely private visits to hospices and Aids clinics were very different from the glittering events of which she was so often the centrepiece. She, of all people, knew that patients need their privacy too, so it was for their sakes as well as her own that these visits were unheralded. She seldom talked about this work. Sometimes when I saw her after a particularly harrowing night she might say a little, but in the main she just got on with things and didn't expect to be sympathized with, let alone congratulated. Equally, she was not at all holier-than-thou about it, nor was she judgemental, for instance, of Fergie's lack of interest in this sort of low-profile work. Even though they had quarrelled Diana still had some regard for her former sister-in-law, seeing her as hasty and misled rather than intrinsically flawed, and referring to Fergie as one of the most generous people she knew. Gone, however, were the days when the two women would time their colonic irrigation sessions so that they would be in different rooms of the same clinic at the same time, and then giggle together afterwards, perhaps about their different expectations of the treatment. Fergie hoped to lose weight, while Diana saw her colonics as therapy and as a time for cleansing, energizing and also rest. She needed her strength for her private visits to the homeless, the sick and the dying as much as for anything else.

Diana was absolutely determined that her boys should be prepared in every respect for the world in which they were, and are, both destined to play important parts. To this end she would sometimes take them to hostels and hospices, squats and council houses, so that by her example they would learn that not everyone has a safe place to call home, a loving family, good food on the table, a job, money in the pocket and robust health. Perhaps these excursions were baffling at times for William and Harry, but Diana wanted them to learn young that their privileges were indeed extraordinary. If nothing else, those visits with their mother proved to the young princes that the disadvantaged matter just as much as those who live in ease and comfort. Above all, she showed them that certain things they may have felt to have been theirs by right are not to be taken for granted. In this she bestowed on her sons a great humanitarian gift which should serve them well, whatever their futures might hold. It seems, too, that their father, Prince Charles, has taken these principles closer to his heart since Diana was killed, and will do the best he can to ensure that the ideals she lived for, fought for and died with are only the marvellous beginnings of a passionate campaign which will be followed through under his guidance.

9

The Men in Her Life

For a long time Diana had felt particularly bitter about her husband's mistress of many years, Camilla Parker Bowles, finding it baffling as well as hurtful that one woman, especially a Cancerian like herself, could behave so deceitfully towards another. Until as late as 1992, eleven years after her marriage, Diana had been forced to meet Mrs Parker Bowles socially, sometimes in public, and to feign a gracious oblivion about the intense love affair between Camilla and the Prince of Wales. Such occasions were indeed ordeals. Diana was almost as angered by the fact that Charles's family knew what was happening and tacitly accepted the state of affairs. They had never embraced Diana in the same way, but only as a brood mare who had dutifully safeguarded the future of the Windsor dynasty by producing two sons.

She remained inarticulately angered at Charles's inability to understand her as a woman and respond to her vulnerability. Like many others, I believe that Diana's affair with James Hewitt, which began in the late 1980s, was at heart a pathetic and misguided attempt to fight back, and that at any time up to their divorce her greatest wish was for reconciliation with her husband. If Charles had offered her just enough kindness, support and affection, I am convinced that Diana would have been adult enough to tolerate his parallel need for Camilla. Whether she would have been underselling herself in such a situation must remain for ever a moot point. What is certain, however, is that Diana felt a growing resentment at Charles's apparent inability to display loyalty towards her in the face of disparaging comments from family and friends. Moreover, things were made even worse for her, as is clear from her observation that it was not as if her husband was unaware of her misery. Various remarks he made proved that he saw it very clearly, but instead of showing that he was worried about her, he would ask his friends to take care of her, proving himself guiltily incapable of acknowledging his wife's pain. A few years later a mellowed Diana told me that she actually felt rather sorry for Camilla, adding that she doubted whether Charles, even then, would be able to muster strong support for his mistress if ever she should need it. He had, she said, really no idea how to treat a woman. Indeed, she always felt that Prince Charles could never be happy with just one woman, and rather agreed with Sir James Goldsmith's dictum that when you marry your mistress you create a job vacancy.

Diana had tried to be beautiful for Charles. She had tried to take an interest in polo, in the environment, in so many aspects of his life and work, to please him. She had even tried to like Balmoral, the place which she would for ever associate with the miserable realization, only weeks after her wedding, that her marriage was unlikely to be a happy one (although she rather liked Scotland). She tried to make Highgrove at least as much of a home as Kensington Palace. Although she abominated blood sports she did not try to prevent her sons from following their father's interest here, laughingly referring to William and Harry when she spoke of this to me as the 'Killer Wales', with a strange mixture of humour and regret. But nothing worked and she felt she had failed yet again.

I believe that Diana had formed a strong interest in the paranormal when she was a schoolgirl and had at least read about it since. She was, too, a great believer in astrology, tending always, for instance, to be very wary of people whose birthsign was Leo because she feared they would take the spotlight away from her. Her interest was reignited when she and her sister-in-law Sarah, Duchess of York, found that they had this in common. It wasn't much of a surprise or a departure, therefore, when Diana first began to visit psychics and mediums in the late 1980s, in the hopes of divining ways of getting Charles back and to see if there was any future for their marriage. These hopes persisted as late as 1995. Indeed, Diana and I had the first of our brief but intense quarrels when I upset her by telling her, not what she wanted to hear, but that she was deluding herself about this. I had no problem with that generous instinct of hers which made her seek never to blame Charles for the breakdown of the marriage, but there was, I said, no point in hoping for fundamental change and she should let go. My principal wish was for Diana to stop blaming herself and thus to begin to mend.

As I have said, after the *Panorama* programme the Queen had contacted her and Prince Charles to insist that they divorce. Diana had been devastated. By then she had been speaking to psychics for some years, and many predicted that she and Charles would get back together, something Diana had always secretly wanted, dreaming that one day her husband would come back on his knees to beg her forgiveness and ask to make a new start. Like so many of her dreams, it was unrealistic and fanciful. When she had to face the bitter truth from the Queen, Diana fell apart. She couldn't sleep at night and started taking very strong sleeping pills. She was constantly in tears, reflecting over and over on what might have been.

In truth, she had been little more than a child bride. Having been denied a 'normal' childhood, whatever that might be, it isn't really surprising that she felt the need to play out the childish bafflements, tantrums, tempers and foot-stampings when she was a very young woman. The fact that she was sexually innocent is also relevant. She was steered into marriage both early and inexperienced. It never surprised me that Diana had some catching-up to do or that she sometimes chose to do so with the wrong men. I'd sensed a great deal of this but it was with relief—on both sides, I think—that Diana eventually began to talk about things. She never gave me elaborate explanations or excuses about her brace of doomed romantic obsessions—but eventually she told me enough to enable me to offer appropriate sympathy.

It is a great shame that Diana's mistakes were always so subject to scrutiny by the press and public. Most of us can be fairly certain that our adolescent crushes and indiscretions will be forgotten or, if remembered at all, will be regarded with a fond tolerance. Diana, ten years or more older than most people when they make their first teenaged blunders, and in the glare of the world's flashbulbs, had not a hope of this. She was forced to grow up in public and no one had taught her how to cope. I like to hope that I steered her away from some potential embarrassments; equally, I would never have sought to spare or

shelter her from the few heady excitements that her short
life belatedly offered her.

By 1986, she barely in her mid-twenties, the physical
spark was extinguished from her marriage. As it ground
on many of Diana's frustrations became apparent, as did
her plunging sorrow that Charles not only did not care to
try to understand her faltering grasp on the duties which
had been imposed upon her, but also simply could not
recognize that she had any reason to be unhappy. Given
his strange and contradictory training, with its emphasis
on invincibility and service, he probably thought Diana
should count herself lucky. It was certainly at best tact-
less, and at worst wilfully cruel, when, earlier in the
marriage, he had observed his wife toying, or sometimes
struggling, with a family meal and remarked loudly that
he wondered when the food was going to re-emerge. Remarks about wastage could scarcely have made her feel
any better about herself, or encouraged her to keep the
food down.

It was particularly hurtful for Diana that Charles's
family knew so much about her self-destructive ways of
dealing with her pain and yet showed little concern and
offered virtually no support. She would have found this
far less upsetting if she'd been able to believe that they
were ignorant of her plight. Their dismissive attitude to
her problems confused and upset her. She already had a
fairly strong suspicion that she was valued amongst them
only as the mother of the future heir to the throne and
now this attitude confirmed things. She was further distressed when she realized that her husband's family were
well aware that while she was suffering, Charles was
happily hunting and otherwise relaxing with the wife of
one of his closest friends, Camilla Parker Bowles.

Diana's stresses were greatly increased by public duties and charity or other obligations. The pressure upon her to be glamorous, caring and reliable did not diminish even as she struggled with the anguish inside her. She never let anyone down as Princess of Wales, but this made it more and more inevitable that, in private, she would need to express her pain. In the worst times of self-mutilation this had gone dangerously far beyond secluded days of sobbing and the black hole of depression—endlessly raking over the same old ground in her mind, wondering why and where she had failed. She assumed all the guilt, without quite knowing what exactly she had done wrong. It is a sad irony that, later, Diana would place friends who had transgressed her codes in the same uncomfortable position of knowing that they had displeased her, somehow, but unable to attempt to make amends because their 'crime' was never explained. Equally, it is to her credit that she only ever expressed bafflement to me about the situation with Camilla Parker Bowles—not hatred or anger, although some of her friends were furious about Charles and Camilla, and spoke to the press about the treatment of Diana. She, however, behaved with a wounded dignity that occasionally expressed itself in tears but seldom in venom towards either Charles or Camilla.

This, again, is typical behaviour for a person who was once a lonely, emotionally neglected—if not actually rejected—child. I was so relieved, therefore, to see Diana gradually swing back towards philosophical acceptance and, by 1996, to have watched her recover herself and, finally, feel some release, even exultation, when the divorce proceedings were completed. Indeed, from that point onwards she and Charles were able to communicate with an honest affection they had never shared before.

Diana had told me that she had wanted Charles to seek therapy with her during those last months of the marriage when she still maintained some faint hopes that things might be rescued. He had dismissed the idea out of hand, however—influenced, Diana believed, by the small group of uncritical friends in whom he confided. Divorce was a far cleaner solution for hopeless marital troubles than the one they had tried to steer him towards before— that of having Diana committed to the velvet prison of some discreet residential clinic. It is revealing of Charles that he even considered this option—one which would have simultaneously hidden the 'problem' and released him from any responsibility for it. If his wife was officially declared deranged, what else could he have done? For her part, Diana told me that things might have been tolerable before their separation if only she had received some understanding and a few affectionate hugs from Charles at crucial times. A husband's thoughtful and caring nod back to the psychological difficulties experienced by numbers of his own recent ancestors might also have helped. His Great-Uncle John, an epileptic who died as a young man, was considered to be so mentally inadequate as to embarrass the royal family, and lived most of his short life with nurses in a cottage on the Sandringham estate. In his maternal grandmother's family two elderly female relatives were quietly consigned to a psychiatric hospital and his grandfather, King George VI, stammered so badly that therapists were called to help him overcome this psychologically rooted affliction.

Diana knew her husband well enough to realize that he, too, had been a victim, the sort of damaged person that her caring impulses naturally reached out towards. Yet even in refusing to recognize this, Charles had rejected and crushed her yet again. He did, however, try to assume or borrow from her some of the qualities which had made her so popular as the Princess of Wales and which he wanted to emulate and perhaps even to trump. With his high-profile Prince's Trust, launched before his marriage and forged to encourage endeavour amongst otherwise disadvantaged young people, he earned a few points—if not much real credibility. He often seemed uneasy at rock concerts staged to raise funds for his Trust, stiffly and unconvincingly attempting to seem to be an ordinary sort of bloke, while being much more at ease when he was discussing philosophy, the opera or modern architecture with the highbrow flatterers he preferred to be with. It was notable how, when the two of them attended Prince's Trust rock concerts together, Diana seemed genuinely to enjoy the music and the atmosphere and was clearly at ease during the informalities with performers after the show. Charles's face throughout, however, was strained, almost pained, as he attempted to appreciate the music whilst snapping his fingers hopelessly out of time or fiddling with the knot of his tie. His unease with informality can be seen in a revealing photograph of the Waleses having a picnic in the grounds of Highgrove, taken by Lord Snowdon, a 'relaxed' family portrait in the manner of a Reynolds or Gainsborough painting. Charles wears a double-breasted suit and his concession to informality is the absence of a tie and the undone top button of his shirt.

Moreover, the considerable achievements of the Prince's Trust might well be attributed, at least in part, to Charles's need to compete with his wife in this sort of area of public service. Tragically, however, he vetoed Diana's wish to set up her own Princess of Wales Trust, perhaps needlessly seeing it as some kind of thunder-stealing opposition rather than a complementary enterprise. It is as though he was quite unable to grasp the basic principles of partnership in which any good marriage is grounded. Indeed, he was so obsessed with his superiority in the relationship that he allegedly even stooped to replacing the 'we' in thank-you letters drafted by Diana on behalf of both of them with 'I'.

One of many differences between them might be that while Diana could admit, however painfully, that her childhood had been less than ideal, and was thus truly able to empathize with victims and sufferers, Charles had endured a different but equally chilling kind of family life, schooling and upbringing, coupled with the fatal instillation of a sense of his own unassailable importance and destiny. A product of this sort of education is unlikely to be sensitive and sympathetic to the flaws and needs of others. After all, if he had managed to overcome his problems, why shouldn't everyone else? So just as Diana was moved, even impelled, to repair, to make everything better, to heal, Charles was primed to imagine that his very presence was sufficient inspiration to people to get them moving and, perhaps, that they should be grateful to him into the bargain because, however patronizingly, he was taking some sort of interest. Diana's hopes that Charles would take a sincere interest in grassroots problems in society were probably always doomed because he was used to his cotton-wool cocoon, didn't really want to step away from it and was, in any case, encouraged to remain insulated from life's realities by sycophantic friends.

Long after their separation, Diana was prone to grim mood swings and temper tantrums. Her despondency might last for days and although she never cancelled an official engagement, her friends could be fair game. Once she rang me, trying to cancel an evening plan, saying that she wasn't fit for human company, looked terrible and felt totally worthless, so why should I bother to come and see her? I had to ask her if she thought I'd mind if she wasn't looking her best and if she honestly thought she was the only woman in history who'd felt miserable and depressed. I pointed out that it is at times like this that we need our friends the most. She paused, and then that pendulum of hers swung again. She asked me to come right over to Kensington Palace after all and within minutes I was on my way. She opened the door to me with red, puffy eyes and cheeks smudged with mascara. I listened and gave her loads of sympathy, she had a good restorative cry and, for the time being, she felt better. But it was another year before such mood swings all but disappeared.

Initially, Diana was dreadfully upset when, in 1994, stories circulated about 'Tiggy' Legge-Bourke, the young woman whom Charles had engaged to care for the boys in their mother's absence. There were pictures of Tiggy with William and Harry on the slopes during skiing holidays in Switzerland, and the nanny added to Diana's anger and distress by saying that she thought the boys regarded her as something of a surrogate mother. There was, moreover, that famous picture of Prince Charles kissing her on the cheek. In a state of heightened anxiety Diana even wondered whether Charles and Tiggy had developed a close friendship themselves. But while the Prince was undoubtedly fond of Tiggy, I'm sure that

Diana's fears that she had yet another enduring rival, this time for her sons' affections as well as her husband's, were unfounded. To some it may seem odd that, after their separation, Diana still thought in terms of rivalry, but many people retain a sense of possessiveness about their exes, even long after a divorce.

In any case, it was her sons who were the focus of Diana's worries. Those initial rumours about Tiggy briefly enraged her. 'They have a mother, she's alive and she's here . . .' she announced. She soon calmed down, however, becoming sanguine, mature and confident again. Diana knew her boys needed to be looked after in her absence and, despite Tiggy's comment, she was utterly sure of her own irreplaceable role in their lives. She knew that the nanny played an important steadying part in the boys' routines as their friend, and that they were fond of her. Her presence could well make weekends spent with their father more fun for William and Harry. But that was all, so that even in her darkest moods Diana recognized that Tiggy was no substitute for her. Even so, this calm and sensible attitude was coloured by a thin veneer of self-protection: for Diana it was more than enough to deal with one other woman in her husband's life—she could not possibly have coped with the idea of two.

She took quite a different view, however, about any relationship between her sons and Camilla Parker Bowles. As far as Diana was concerned, this was not—must not—even be entertained. In this respect she had complete trust in the agreement she had struck with Charles: one day, when their sons were old enough to understand such matters, they would be told about Camilla and the important part she played in Charles's life. But not until then—and there was to be no insidious usurping of Diana's place in the meantime.

Diana wanted desperately to have a daughter.

No mother could have loved her sons more or protected them better, but if there was one unfulfilled ambition in her life, one as yet unrealized hope, it was to have a little girl. Towards the end of her life she saw Hasnat Khan as the potential father of this child, telling me of her daydream about herself and Hasnat as a happily married couple with a brood of children around their feet. It was the same kind of fantasy she had had with Hewitt, who himself admitted that what she had wanted was to settle down with him in the country, helping him with his riding business. I remember, as she was outlining to me her vision of the future with Hasnat Khan, telling her, 'This isn't *EastEnders*, you know. The royal family would never allow you to live like that.'

Even as she entered her mid-thirties Diana knew she still had time on her side—good years—and she wasn't neurotically concerned with the inevitable and natural ageing processes. She took great care of herself, and had no need to worry about facial lines or physical decline. She did, uncharacteristically, fall into depressions about things like those newspaper pictures which apparently showed cellulite around her thighs. Diana had no cellulite and, as I've already said, I believe those pictures, with their 'evidence' of puckering and dimpling, could have been tampered with.

Although the publication of the photos made her exercise even more rigorously, she wasn't generally worried about the still-distant spectre of being forty. Her periods laid her low, but obviously she knew they evidenced her continuing fertility.

Like Elizabeth Taylor, who has tended to formalize her romantic attachments, Diana was essentially the 'marrying kind', and after it became clear that she would divorce she began seriously to think ahead. She often told me that she was sure that she would remarry, even after the blow to her optimism dealt by James Hewitt, and I believe her wish for a daughter was central to this conviction. But even when she was most passionately obsessed with Hasnat she would pause and then shake her head slowly and sadly when I asked her if she could really see herself living quietly and modestly as his wife, with the occasional spurt of campaigning work for heart charities as her only forays into public life.

I'm convinced that her insistence on keeping in the best possible shape was not only from her wish to look her best for her public, but was partly influenced by wanting to be desired by men and to be ready to conceive again with the right man when the time came. One day I went through her medicine cabinets with her, both of us laughing as we examined bottles, boxes, tubes and jars of over-prescribed remedies, sweeping them into plastic bags. Many of the medicines and treatments, recommended by therapists with differing principles and agendas, had barely been sampled, and were in any case long past their use-by dates. I told Diana yet again that with her careful, balanced and largely organic diet she had little need for such supplements. Some extra vitamin C seldom does anything but good, but many of the potions that she was discarding were little better than junk. Somewhere along the line Diana had formed the idea that she had a wheat allergy and needed dietary supplements as well as a gluten-free eating regime. I advised her to dump these complicating 'nutritional supplements' too.

The aromatic oils she used in her bath were sometimes ones she had specially mixed for her and at others simply bought from Penhaligon. Her camomile and mint teas, the invigorating drinks she made for herself in the juicer from combinations of carrot, cucumber, beetroot and celery, and her scented candles all provided the extra energy or relaxation she needed when coupled with her regular diet. Had God—and the right man—been willing, there was absolutely no reason why Diana, brimming with good health and vitality, could not have had another child.

In the meantime she had her boys. There was never any doubt that their happiness and well-being were her first priorities, and from the moment of her separation from Prince Charles she coped quite brilliantly with the stresses of being a single mother. At the time when I came to know her best William was beginning to suffer the inevitable complications of adolescence—difficult enough in ordinary circumstances, but especially so if parents are divorcing. Harry, although still young enough to be spared these trials, was as upset by his parents' separation and impending divorce as any other little boy would have been. Diana's tactile and honest approach to the young princes must have helped them both immeasurably and I thought she handled this delicate situation with great intelligence and sensitivity. That they get on so well with their father is partly due to Diana's policy of never speaking unfairly of Charles to the boys.

Even though, in term time, Diana could only see her sons one weekend in five and was always thrilled in anticipation of a couple of days with them, she never stifled them when they were with her. Unless she had attended a school function between their weekends together, she would not have seen them for over a month—a long, long time for a woman whose children were utterly pivotal to her own good spirits and well-being, and who could only guess about what newspaper-fed stories and rumours they had had to deal with since she saw them last. She tried to keep up regular telephone contact each day during those weeks of separation. William had a pager so that he could respond to the 'ring Mummy' messages she left for him as soon as there was an appropriate moment. But she wasn't intrusive, and their times together with their mother were as important for the boys as they were for her. She would seldom answer the phone during those weekends, or even take calls. On the occasions when I rang it was normally William who picked up. He was invariably friendly and polite, although the first time we spoke he was inquisitive enough to ask me where I lived and whether I was married, or had a boyfriend. The curiosity wasn't the least bit offensive—it merely reflected his mother's genuine interest in the lives of other people. As for Harry (whom she'd asked me to scan once, when he was feeling poorly), after I'd first met him he apparently told his mother, with astonishing youthful insight, 'I bet that lady likes cats, candles and crystals.'

Wanting to surprise Diana for Christmas in 1996, the boys asked Paul for ideas for a present for her, and he in turn asked me. I was stumped for a moment, and clichés like *What do you give to the woman who has everything?* rushed to mind. Then I remembered telling the Princess about my amethyst cave and how interested she had seemed. This is a large, heavy, grey rock—quite beautiful in its own right—which has been cleanly cracked in half to reveal a hollow interior encrusted with the most stunning purple crystals, light refracting from the facets of each one. The rock balances steadily, both sides of its crystal cave generating energies as well as beauty and light. These rocks come in all sizes and can be obtained from a few specialist shops in England. I pointed the boys in the right direction and heard later from Diana that they had found her an enormous and particularly lovely amethyst cave, a present she was to treasure.

Employees at Kensington Palace usually worked a five-day week, but on those weekends when the boys were at home the staff would come in, unobtrusively, and deal with domestic chores, while Diana would ensure that she had no official or even social commitments. If the weekend was to be spent largely at Kensington Palace, William and Harry didn't mind. Diana was wise enough to know that it would have been poor training for them if they could only associate time with their mother with extraordinary treats. Besides, all three of them wanted to bask in some rare and private normality whenever possible, and any outings they went on were likely to be publicized—William was, and remains, particularly uneasy about intrusive behaviour by the media. Evenings were usually spent watching TV, or just talking and laughing and catching up.

The boys had their own rooms, as well as a separate sitting room close to Diana's suite where they could play their own music and computer games. But they spent most of the time with their mother in absolutely unforced relaxation. Just as she had loved to get down on the carpet to romp with and cuddle them when they were much younger—and still played like this with her many younger godchildren—she really enjoyed her sons' company, and their sense of humour. Harry still loved sitting on her lap and snuggling his head into her neck, as I noticed when I was there.

Like any other proud, classically love-blinded mother, Diana maintained that her sons were always beautifully behaved, and never quarrelled or were otherwise difficult or naughty. If this was completely true then William and Harry must have been the first teenaged boys in history to be such paragons, but I must say I always found them both to be friendly, charming, and unaffectedly well mannered. The only time I was aware of Diana's confidence in their perfect grace and goodness faltering was when she told me how upset she'd been by a remark Harry had made about 'other men'. When she had told her sons about Hasnat, the younger prince's reaction had led her to suppose that it had been too early, for him, at least, to have met the surgeon. The older William had taken a more adult point of view.

It was certainly a delicate situation. Young boys are not renowned for the sophistication of their wit, Hasnat himself had implied to Diana that he wasn't ready to become a surrogate father to two teenagers, and she had to prove to her sons that they were her absolute priority. As a result, this romantic aspect of her life was held in complete suspense while the boys were with her. I'm sure it would have been the same if Diana's love life had centred around an English duke, an American mogul or a European prince: whoever the man was the boys were going to be unsettled, given their parents' separation. At Christmas 1995, when Diana asked the boys what presents they wanted, both of them had asked for their father to come back home.

There were always children's pictures and paintings on display in Diana's dressing room and bathroom, many sent to her by beneficiaries of her charities. She just knew how to communicate with children, and there was nothing artificial or strained in her ease with her sons and her understanding of their youthful concerns. As well as naturally falling into 'man-about-the-house' mode with his mother, William was extraordinarily protective of his young brother, rather than finding him tiresome as many boys of his age might have done. I came to realize that the princes really were well behaved and, given their circumstances, amazingly well adjusted. Squabbles were very rare, not least because they genuinely enjoyed each other's company.

One of Diana's evenings at home with the boys was particularly riotous when together they watched the televised debate on the future of the monarchy, broadcast in January 1997. I was watching at home, but was on the phone to Diana throughout (we were on the phone for eight hours that day!). Using one of her four mobiles, Diana was on the phone the whole day ringing friends such as Rosa Monckton, Cosima Somerset and Richard Kay, urging them to vote against the royal family in the phone poll that formed a key part of the programme. In fact, the following day Richard rather sheepishly confessed that he had cast his vote for the monarchy, arguing that they brought in tourist revenues. Diana was not at all amused that he had not voted against her 'in-laws'.

She told me the House of Windsor would not be getting her vote, explaining, 'They have to learn what it is like for ordinary people. What on earth would they think if there were a revolution? They don't know what hard work means.' She herself was one of the first to register her vote in the phone-in. Throughout the evening she pressed her redial button, registering something like two hundred and fifty votes against the monarchy. At one point William scolded her, saying, 'Haven't you got anything better to do with your money? Just think of all the sweets you could buy.' That evening also gave me an insight into Prince William's thinking about his future role. When the programme was debating whether the young prince should become King he said emphatically, 'I don't want the job.' However, he also made it clear that if he did succeed to the throne, he would sell off some of the royal palaces. A young man with a well-developed social conscience, thanks to his mother's training, he could not reconcile his own privileges with the difficult lives endured by so many of his future subjects.

There was one particularly awkward moment when the show's host, Trevor McDonald, asked the audience to vote on whether Camilla Parker Bowles should become Queen. Young Prince Harry, cuddled up to his mother on the sofa, piped up with 'Who is Camilla?' Hurriedly, Diana said that it was time for him to go to bed, bribing him with a plate of chips to get him out of the room.

It was William who had the idea of the charity sale of some of Diana's most spectacular designer dresses. His demand for 10 per cent of the take was not, however, received with the same enthusiasm. He was becoming quite interested in all matters relating to style and fashion, reaching the age when he wanted to choose his own clothes and go shopping for them, rather than allow Diana to pick everything out for him. She understood this and ensured that the financial side of such expeditions was properly arranged via the detective who always discreetly accompanied him. Equally, if William wanted to spend a few hours with other schoolfriends, shopping or simply lounging in a café, and so long as his minder kept an eye on him from a tactful distance, Diana was happy for him to go out alone and spend his pocket money as he pleased. There must have been times when he was recognized, but so far as I know he was never troubled. One has to remember that William's suddenly matured face became much more familiar to the public at large after Diana's funeral, and also that around the environs of Kensington Palace, where he usually shopped or met friends, he had been out and about with his mother since he was very young and was thus not a particularly unusual sight.

Neither William nor Harry was around to see their mother's distress as she helped to catalogue her dresses for the auction that her elder son had suggested. While relieved in a way to dispatch these sumptuous symbols of a miserable recent past, Diana was inevitably upset by this very practical way of letting go. Some happy memories—at least of hopes and expectations—must have attached to some of the gowns. She told me her memories of each of them as I sat with her and was often rather waspish, saying that this dress was 'absolutely dreadful' or that another one was too 'fairy-tale princess'. But I know that she had wept before she finally relinquished them, and photographs taken of her modelling dresses for the sale catalogue at the time had to be airbrushed to remove the red-eyed signs of recent weeping. No number of cold tea bags or cucumber slices pressed against her eyelids that morning could disguise the evidence of a long, tearful night.

In 1996 William confided to Diana that he wanted to send a Valentine card to the model Cindy Crawford, for whom he'd developed something of an admiration. I'm not quite sure why, but Diana thought she'd better check with Ms Crawford's office to ensure that this would be all right; perhaps she wanted to ensure that her boy's message would at least reach somewhere near the top of the stack of fan mail that the supermodel was bound to receive at such a time. She was given the OK, and William's card was duly acknowledged with a signed photograph.

Diana was so reassuring to William when he was going through the embarrassing agonies of his voice breaking—'Don't worry, Wombat, it's normal,' she told him. She was also very sensitive in the way she explained to him about what to expect as his body went through the various stages of puberty. With the slightly but crucially younger Harry such skills were not yet necessary.

William could be equally reassuring to his mother, however. When she had the HRH title stripped from her by the Queen she was initially bothered about having to bow and scrape to Princess Michael, her next-door neighbour, whom she heartily disliked. But then William put it all into persepective for her: 'It doesn't matter whether you have a title. To us you are still our mummy.'

Both boys were tremendously fond of and caring towards the Princesses Beatrice and Eugenie, and often spent time with them during their weekends out from school until Diana had her quarrel with Fergie late in 1996. These cousins were the only ones the boys were particularly close to at that time, partly because of age differences. Contact with the others wasn't much encouraged after Diana and Charles had separated, although she always remembered former in-laws' birthdays with cards and gifts, especially the Queen, Prince Philip, Princess Margaret and Princess Anne. Diana told me about phoning the Queen after her birthday in 1996, not having received acknowledgement of her present, and listening as Her Majesty described how marvellous it was to have received so many gifts from all over the world. In her telling of the story, Diana said she waited for a pause in this account of it all before mischievously interjecting, 'But isn't it nice to get presents from people who really love you?'

In a way Diana was reaching out for bonds far beyond those of traditional family and in-laws. Her friendships—although, as has been shown, she didn't always handle these with perfect maturity or finesse—were increasingly important to her, and it gave her particular pleasure when a new friendship seemed to embrace her whole family. Long before May 1997, when Tony Blair's Labour Party won the General Election, Diana had become genuinely fond of the future Prime Minister and his wife, Cherie, but it gave her extra pleasure to see how well her sons got on with the Blairs' children when things were relaxed and political matters forgotten over a meal or an afternoon together. Had she been able to, I'm certain that Diana would have voted for the Labour Party; she was so much in sympathy with its election manifesto.

Sometimes, of course, the princes would want a meal in a fast-food restaurant or to go to see a mindless movie and Diana would usually oblige. Given the strictness and care with which she monitored her own food intake, she had a very relaxed, progressive and intelligent attitude towards her sons' diet and did not seek to deny them fast or junk foods, in case the boys should come to regard them as extra-special treats and gorge on them in later life. The last thing she wanted to instil in them was the neurotic idea that mealtimes could be a chore or a bore, nor did she want to make a 'big deal' about either virtuous foods or forbidden ones. She knew that growing children need carbohydrates and sugars, and also that if they ate their fill of burgers and ice creams now they would be unlikely to develop cravings for them when they were older.

Food for the boys at home might have been sent out for or prepared in the KP kitchen. A video might be borrowed. But if they went out to a cinema in Kensington or Knightsbridge they would probably have a burger or pizza in a quiet corner of a restaurant, their arrival sometimes surprising the proprietors of such places. Because of the boys two detectives would be in unobtrusive attendance. There would usually be a stop at McDonald's towards the end of the weekend to ease the normal schoolboy dislike of returning to boarding school. William and Harry were both quite happily settled but it must have been a wrench to return to the prospect of double maths or whatever after such lovingly indulgent weekends.

Diana simply couldn't spend as much time as she would have liked to with her sons. She adored children in any case, which I think was one of the reasons why she maintained links with some children's charities even after her semi-withdrawal from public life in 1995 made it necessary, that July, for her to cut her ties with many of the charities with which she had been connected before. Although it was drastically curtailed, Diana still took her charity work very seriously.

She would stoop to ask the name of every child she met during a formal or informal engagement, and she would remember it. During her private visits to the Great Ormond Street Hospital for Sick Children, or the Brompton, she would sit beside a young patient and talk, cool a fevered face with a damp cloth or try to offer support to worried parents. She sometimes visited Great Ormond Street as often as three times a week, arriving unannounced and figuratively rolling up her sleeves. If there was nothing else to do she would deal with the dead flowers and arrange any fresh ones. I am sure that all this did much for Diana's self-esteem because it really made her feel part of an important and useful team; she never tried to interfere with what medical and nursing staff were doing, however. She simply and quietly tried to help in her own way and by now she had the confidence to accept what she could do: offer a kind of healing by her touch, her words and her presence. Diana approached this work with thoughtful care, wearing tactile fabrics like velvet if she was visiting blind people, and always remembering to place a dangly pendant round her neck if she was visiting babies so that there was something bright and pretty for them to reach up to and clutch as she bent to them.

It was the same when she visited a hospice or a unit where people with Aids were being cared for. She would have done her homework, read about the most recent developments concerning the condition of a particular patient she wanted to speak to and empathize with. Her own childhood suffering had, ironically, equipped her so well for this work. I am absolutely convinced that Diana, if she had a choice, would want to be remembered for her work in hospitals and hospices, rather than with another public garden. Londoners are fortunate enough to have many such lovely places already.

With her boys away most of the time, her mother in Scotland, her father dead, one sister virtually off-limits and the other understandably preoccupied with her own young brood, Diana was missing family life dreadfully in the months before she died. Even the most beautiful or celebrated person has to realize, sometimes with pain, that for even the dearest of friends, family must come first. And so at times—especially at weekends, when families spend time together, often leaving town altogether—she could be especially lonely. She had misread the signs when she tried to get more involved with one particular family, and felt saddened and rejected when they made it clear that they felt her interest in them bordered upon intrusion. She had not always handled her friendships well, so there were really very few people she could count on. At least there were still regular Sunday lunches with the Goldsmith family, but however warm their welcome, Diana was still a guest.

And when I remember the interest she showed in my own family, the extraordinary pleasure we took in the coincidence that she had met my sister Rachel years before at a hospital in Northampton, her support for me when my father died and her kindness towards my mother . . . all of these things and more, I regret so deeply that the opportunity never quite arose for her to come to North London for that home-cooked family dinner which she and my mother discussed. It might not have been the most exciting or glamorous of evenings for her, but during one of those weekends when she was alone in Kensington Palace and missing her boys, I know she would have been glad of the simple and affectionate welcome she would certainly have received.

Of course, I couldn't help wondering what Diana would have thought about the announcement, in July 1998, that William had met Camilla Parker Bowles at last, and that after the first meeting a week earlier two or three more had taken place in Prince Charles's apartments in St James's Palace. Knowing what I did of William—that he has an inquisitive nature, a tendency that Diana had always encouraged—I cannot but think that the meeting would have been the young prince's idea. He has never been one to be forced into anything he isn't ready for or is unwilling to undertake. It seems likely now, as I write, that Camilla will shortly begin to form a relationship with Harry, too. He's an inquisitive boy, too, and is bound to have discussed the meeting with his big brother.

Tiggy Legge-Bourke may also have primed them. The boys are far too grown-up to need a nanny these days but Tiggy remains a great friend and companion, and one who, for many years now, has often been around during their visits to their father. Despite initial and wholly understandable—albeit unnecessary—worries about being somehow usurped by Tiggy, Diana came to value her steady presence and the strong sense of continuity she gave to the boys. This represented a very marked change from the attitude she had voiced years earlier. Then it had been bad enough for her to contemplate another woman in her husband's life, and so doubly difficult to fear a replacement for herself as mother as well. But that stage passed. Tiggy must have had to answer many sensitive questions from her young charges and Diana trusted her to do so appropriately. One way and another, by

1998 the young princes were ready to take the inevitable step of getting to know Mrs Parker Bowles.

But naturally the most important and influential factor in the way that William and Harry will deal with their father's life, and the other people central to it, came from Diana and what she told them, especially in the last months before her death when she and Charles began to talk again. They spoke as civilized, affectionate adults, above and beyond the conflicts and wounds both had endured and inflicted. Their conversations ranged widely, their views and opinions shared as between equals. Charles and Diana were *friends* at long last. And if that friendship was complicated, it was also bound by the deepest common interest of all—their unqualified love and concern for their sons.

I'm often asked if I think that the boys will suffer any psychological scarring from their parents' divorce and Diana's death. It is a question to which I can give no easy answer. Obviously, they will have been deeply affected, particularly Prince Harry. While William has grown up into a very mature and strong-willed young man, his brother is still a little boy. As I've said, I remember how he used to love cuddling up to his mother on the sofa, Diana cradling him gently in the crook of her arm. 'It's so nice when William is not here, I can spend all my time with you,' he would say. It is worth noting, too, that not only Diana, but also Charles, made it a rule never to say anything wounding about each other to their sons. It was a compact between them. The same cannot be said of Charles's friends, however—often the boys would tell Diana about derogatory comments made by some of the people close to their father.

If the British monarchy can survive it will depend to a

great extent on Prince William. Both his parents m
take credit for the fact that as a young man he sho
every sign of having the grace and character to be a tru
modern king. Prince Charles, it is said, once wanted
daughter as much as Diana did. That may be one of th
most tragic ironies surrounding the end of their mar
riage. On the birth of Harry in 1984 there were many
easy, flippant remarks about his being 'the spare', and no
child or young man with any spirit will not resent such a
silly label at times. But again, I believe that the combination of Diana's even-handed devotion and Charles's intelligent sensitivity will mean that Harry, too, will be
prepared to play a great role in our new century.

Diana's wishes and dreams for her boys are probably
safe. Her wish and dream that they might one day have
had a sister is safe, too, in a Never-Never Land sort of way.

10

Landmines and Letting Go

Even as the terms of their divorce were being hammered out, during what was for both of them a personal winter that lasted for half of 1996, Charles and Diana were beginning to come to a sort of fond accommodation. While their respective lawyers may have fought bitterly, the two principals were speaking to each other with more warmth than for years—perhaps with greater warmth than ever before.

Released, now, from any pretence that they had, or even could have, a marriage, they were free to explore the possibilities of friendship. And since Diana, too, was in love—with Hasnat Khan—most of her old resentment about Camilla Parker Bowles had diminished and she and Charles could see each other's best qualities more clearly than ever before.

When Sir Laurens van der Post, Prince Charles's mentor and friend, and also godfather to Prince William, died in 1996, Diana wrote to Charles a carefully worded letter of heartfelt sympathy, telling him that she above all others knew how devastated he must be feeling. Charles responded immediately, not in the royal way with a formal note but with a touched and emotional phone call. The door was opened for a dialogue that was to continue until Diana died. To me, it suggests that Charles's immediate, stricken, response to her death—flying to Paris to bring her body home later that day—and his reactions in the days that followed were absolutely sincere.

The growing closeness between Charles and Diana continued in the run-up to Christmas 1996 when they both attended events at their boys' schools. Before William's carol service at Eton Diana and Charles were heard laughing together with the Headmaster in his private office. After the service at Harry's school but before driving away Diana called me from her car. I heard a shriek of mirth and she said she'd have to call me back. When she did so she explained that Charles had suddenly appeared and tapped at her car window. Her unstifled peal of laughter had been because she suddenly thought that in his immaculate brown suit and shiny brown shoes he looked just like Fred Astaire, and an image of him breaking into a tap routine had rushed unbidden to her mind. It had been expected that they would mingle with other parents afterwards, but Diana made her excuses to Charles, who ruefully agreed with her that this looked as though it would be a tedious business, and rather nobly agreed to shoulder the duty by himself. This was said, Diana told me, with a good humour that would have been unimaginable only the Christmas before.

A few days later there was a knock on the front door of Diana's Kensington Palace apartments. The member of staff who opened it was startled to see Prince Charles outside. He happened to be passing, he said, and wondered if he could pop in to use the loo. (I had to hope that he was not directed to the lavatory which Diana had decorated with countless framed cartoons of him, not all of them flattering by any means.) Since Diana was at home she greeted him, and as a result he stayed for what proved to be the first of many more easy, informal conversations. By now the divorce had been finalized for some months; as far as the couple were concerned these were private talks, quite separate from the harsh practicalities over which their lawyers had so expensively haggled.

Obviously their principal topic of mutual interest was the welfare of their boys, not merely in the context of the divorce, but also in that of their futures in the broadest terms. The conversations ranged into many other areas, however, and Charles might have been surprised and pleased to discover that these days he could speak to Diana as an equal. She had grown up so much since their separation, and had acquired the self-confidence to articulate her interest in matters philosophical, social, ecological, political and cultural. I've no doubt that at times each of them must have felt a passing twinge of tender regret for what might have been during some of these meetings at Kensington Palace.

In some ways, as she and Charles talked of matters close to his heart during this period of private mutual recovery, Diana was reverting to an old habit, one which I doubt if she would ever have been able or willing to break free of completely. In these conversations she engaged with him as an equal about *his* preoccupations and passions: I would have hoped that Charles took the same interest in Diana's concerns for the world's loveless, wounded and abandoned. It had been the same in the past. Her mind was something of a sponge or a great white sheet of blotting paper, crying out to be filled or imprinted with the passions of the men she loved so that she could share these interests and thereby come to understand the man. Diana had had little interest in horses until she met James Hewitt, or in Middle Eastern art until she knew Oliver Hoare, while her admittedly existing interest in heart disease had increased enormously when she met Hasnat Khan.

This is one more reason why Diana's campaign against anti-personnel landmines was so marvellous. It was all her own work, not stimulated by regard for or influenced by any man. She had a proper job at last. That the outraged eyes of the world have been turned to the abomination of landmines, and that legislation to ban their use has been passed, not merely in Britain, but all over the world, may prove to be Diana's most enduring legacy. For although she was only able to make two journeys, to Angola and to Bosnia, her presence was enough to shift the axis of world thinking by the crucial few degrees that were to have a lasting effect.

I went to Bosnia in the early summer of 1996, after my father died, partly driven by complex needs, and partly to visit my friend Morris Power, a Red Cross worker based in Tuzla, where the locals regarded him as a hero. I was appalled by some of the things I saw and learned, and moved by others, not least by the patience, courage and good humour of the people. Sometimes, even now, I hear distinguished senior soldiers—increasingly in a minority, thanks to Diana—saying that anti-personnel landmines are a sad fact of 'life' in times of war. If an isolated pocket of a reduced and beleaguered army has to regroup and protect itself, they argue, the laying of mines can be an essential aid to the ultimate greater good. Having seen some of their victims, I cannot agree. The people there were not allowed to live with dignity, nor were they allowed to die with it.

I was only in Bosnia for about ten days, but I took

powerful images back to London with me, as well as a great many photographs, which I showed to Diana.

'Do you think I could make a difference?' she asked, poring over the pictures, her face pale with shock.

'If you can't, nobody can,' I replied.

Diana wanted to leave for a war zone as soon as possible. But arrangements took longer than she had expected and her frustrations were sometimes evident. Perhaps the delays were because she was travelling as a private citizen, albeit with the Red Cross, and the diplomatic doors did not immediately and effortlessly swing open as once they had. Perhaps they were compounded by her wish to plan a very wide programme of visits to landmine sites. She had wanted to go first to Cambodia, which has the highest concentration of landmines, but this idea was scuppered because of the considerable risk

This cartoon by Peter Maddocks is one of many which Diana hung in a Kensington Palace bathroom.

IF HE HAS SWAPPED HER FOR CAMILLA PARKER BOWLES — DIEGO MARADONA IS NOT THE ONLY ONE WHO NEEDS A DRUG TEST!

of kidnap. So the plans shifted to enable her to go to Angola in February 1997 and to Bosnia a few months later. On both occasions she was to be accompanied by the redoubtable Lord Deedes, writing for the *Daily Telegraph*. He had been warned that the Princess was a 'loose cannon', but remarked afterwards, with typical understatement, that she had acquitted herself well.

She was able to call me most mornings. I think she needed a familiar voice with which to chatter about mindless things before facing another stressful day, but whatever the reason, it was wonderful to hear her. I did my best to fill her in with the sort of silly gossip that always made her laugh. Those calls were not underpinned by a need for reassurance or advice. Unless she had been particularly affected by something she had just witnessed these were, in the main, happy and chatty conversations which usually began with a cheerful 'Angola calling Hendon. Come in Hendon . . .' But these weren't long calls and after a bit of a chat she would sign off in order to address her Red Cross work. Sometimes she would have time to go into what she'd seen the previous day, and to ask about how her visit had been reported back in Britain. Naturally she was well aware that there would be reactions and that her presence would draw the attention— or fire—of the international press. It was what she had intended. In the event, only a very few small-minded journalists were spiteful enough to suggest that Diana had anything else on her agenda while in Angola than to draw the world's attention to the plight of the innocents.

Even though we had quarrelled by the time she went to Bosnia early in August 1997, much of the practical advice I had given her before was applicable and I knew she remembered details about some of the people I had met and whom I knew would be lifted by a visit from her. While there she followed roughly the same route as I had taken. Morris was by then in Tanzania, but coincidentally, while in Tuzla she stayed at the house of his girlfriend and her mother, higher up in the hills, where there was constant electricity and running water.

Lord Deedes, who had been in Angola with Diana and remarked afterwards that she had done well there, wrote much more fulsomely of her after she died, affectionately remembering her sense of humour in such desperate conditions, as well as her commitment to the work. In Bosnia, he said, she had 'the engaging trick of approaching me with one hand behind her back. "Have a gin and tonic?" she would say, watch my face light up in anticipation and then hand over a small bottle of water.'

Diana never flinched, he said, at seeing the horrendous mutilations that landmines had caused, realizing that for many victims the evidence of their injuries *had* to be displayed. And she insisted that interviews with victims should be unhurried—half an hour each at least. She realized that it would add to victims' indignities if their individual stories of suffering were seen to be accounted so similar to dozens of others that they could be rushed. She also understood, as not every journalist does, that a long silence during an interview is as eloquent as a speech; then, 'At some point during the outpouring of grief she would reach out to touch the victim on the hand or the face.' Lord Deedes added that interpreters were not always needed: 'Diana had her own way of breaking through the language barrier.'

Commenting upon remarks of the Dean of Westminster, the Very Reverend Wesley Carr, at Diana's funeral service, in which he had spoken of the Princess as someone for whom from afar we all dared to feel affection, and by whom we were all intrigued, Lord Deedes was struck by the Dean's choice of this last word. '"Intrigued!" That is the word, there is the magic,' he wrote afterwards.

When, in Angola, Diana placed the perspex mask over her face, tightened her chest shield and chatted with the cameramen before walking across minefields, she was, despite the calm, almost conversational image she projected, risking her life for the cause she had come to believe in so passionately. True, the fields had been checked over before her walks, but no one could ever be quite sure . . . A mine that had been missed would have no more respected the foot of the Princess of Wales than that of a local dispossessed farmworker. Diana's sheer physical, nerveless courage in this can never be overestimated.

Diana came home from Bosnia, a free woman now, with every intention of returning to a war zone before long. Why would she not? She was well aware how much her work in Angola had already influenced world opinion. In allowing camera crews to film her at work there she had also displayed the depth of her new self-confidence. She had pushed cameras away, angrily saying 'I think that's enough,' if she felt that filming was becoming too intrusive. She had not cared what the world would think of her when she looked at the camera briefly, her eyes red and swollen with tears, a mutilated child lying cradled in her arms. None of this magnificent work was motivated by self-interest. Nevertheless, since Diana was appearing as a free and independent woman on the world's stage for the first time since her divorce, and after Buckingham Palace had refused to allow her to be given an official ambassadorial role, she could have been forgiven if she experienced moments of personal triumph. Her work in Angola and Bosnia was probably her finest hour—a time when Diana was at last able to give real expression to her deepest instincts and to follow her true priorities.

It would have been very difficult, after that, for anyone—even the sycophants and cronies who still surrounded Prince Charles—to dismiss Diana as a shallow and purposeless young woman whose main concerns were nice dresses, pop music and loopy alternative ideas about health, diet and healing. She, after all, had braved a war zone and a battlefield. Most of them had not.

Diana returned home from Bosnia exhausted. Her presence in a war zone and its immediate concerns had enabled her to suspend her worry about Hasnat for a while, but now she had to face it. Things between them hadn't changed much during her absence, although the planning of her next visit to a landmine-infested area may have taken her mind off this.

'The knowledge is expanding at alarming speed. Watch out world . . .' Diana had written to me in an affectionate note around Christmas time in 1996 (see colour plates). That year I had helped her choose the photograph for her official Christmas card, and I found it interesting that of all the hundreds she could have selected she opted for one of her sons with their cousins Beatrice and Eugenie. By then she had enough self-confidence to be, as it were, an absent presence, rather than an actual one, in the picture. In startling contrast to the relative formality of her official card was the personal one she gave me, addressed to 'a special lady'. Her handwriting here is strong and rounded, with firm, fluent pressure, in noteworthy contrast to earlier notes to me where the writing is less steady and well formed. I was pleased—Diana didn't send many of these personal cards.

For weeks before February 1997 she and I discussed her packing for Angola, although I had already told her that she should take only simple and comfortable T-shirts, blouses, trousers and pumps; she also knew that lots of make-up would be unnecessary. She was there to highlight the suffering victims, not as a clothes horse. She took only one dress—a favourite and pretty spotted one which she had worn many times before and which did very well for the one semi-formal evening engagement that she knew had been lined up. This was in dramatic contrast to the baggage she had taken with her on royal visits in the past. Then there would have been dozens of trunks and cases and an entourage which included a dresser and a hair stylist to help her face the cameras. It was, too, a far, far cry from the woman who had sheepishly admitted to me that stories that she spent more than £3,000 a week on grooming and health care were underestimating things, and who didn't even like to wonder how much more she spent on her clothes every week.

Diana had a proper job at last, and spoke now with the strength and purpose of someone who, having floundered for years, at last felt useful. She knew very well that she was taking extraordinary physical risks when she walked across areas which were being swept for mines, but she wanted to prove her courage to herself and thus show the world not only that she was strong, but that this risk she was taking was necessary and important. Her work certainly woke the world up to the landmines issue, and she could be justifiably proud of that. She herself was so shaken by her experience that she donated a large sum of her own money to the cause.

In their fear that she might prove to be an embarrassing 'loose cannon', or that she might upstage other members of the royal family, Britain's royal establishment had denied Diana her wish, as expressed during the *Panorama* interview, to be appointed as some kind of roving ambassadress. She was now proving to them and to everyone else that she would do it, be it, anyway—on her own terms and in her own way. It was both a form of rebellion and an expression of the proof that she was indeed worthy of the trust that she had once hoped might have been officially bestowed upon her. If people misunderstood and imagined that she had some other agenda they were very wrong: Diana simply wanted to use her high profile and her influence for the greater good. By 1997 she was ready to do so.

She had learned, through years of royal training, to disguise some of her emotions publicly and was usually able to seem poised and calm on camera during the Angola visit. But I sometimes heard the choke in her voice when she described to me the plight and condition of some of the landmine victims. She was still innocent enough to be enraged and baffled about why such atrocities had been allowed to happen. She was appalled by the poverty she saw around her even as she was obliged to be gracious at a reception arranged in her honour in the same area. When she asked me to give her strength, through prayer, to cope with it all I told her that I was always with her spiritually. I do not believe that it is necessary to worship formally to draw comfort from God, and I knew that I could and would pray for Diana in my own way.

With Paul Burrell looking after her, rather than a full back-up team, Diana was travelling as a private citizen and, relatively speaking, on a shoestring. Paul had watched her hairdressers at work often enough to know how she liked her hair to be arranged. She was just about able to remember a time when she had done her own unpacking, shaken out her clothes, and hung up things ready for the next day. She was making her own plans, devising her itineraries and, free at last, was proving how much she could do on her own. In this she was supported by her sense of mission as well as her religious and spiritual faith, and by an inner strength which she had slowly rediscovered over the past few years.

The emotional limpet was rapidly becoming a creature of the past. Upon her return from Angola Diana was already wondering what her next mission should be. Together we discussed this, many of our talks focusing on the dreadful situation of the pathetic beggar children in India who have Aids as a result of having been sold into prostitution, and who will suffer and die unless awareness is raised and help and hope are offered. I believe that this would have been Diana's next major undertaking. Before her death she had realized her true power, and had found the confidence to know that her work could make a difference.

It was time to let go, for both of us, soon after Diana returned from Angola. And it was painful.

Just as there are accidents caused by seemingly insignificant failures, so there are divorces apparently caused by snoring, or by irritating habits with the toothpaste tube or in the kitchen. Everyone knows that the relationship in question has not foundered upon the fact that one party has a tendency to forget to water the plants, or whatever. Such 'crimes' are simply voiced as metaphors for the fact that, for one partner or the other, it is time to move on. That is what happened with me and Diana. I should have foreseen it, since I knew only too well that in the past she had sometimes found it easiest to sever a relationship that had once been important to her by concentrating on and exaggerating out of all proportion some otherwise insignificant misunderstanding.

She had proved so much to herself, and I can understand that my continuing close presence in her life was an uncomfortable reminder of times when she had felt wretched and had been more dependent. Our final estrangement was hurtful enough at the time, but it became infinitely worse after her death. We'd fallen out before, and I saw no reason to worry after that last row that we wouldn't patch things up. But we ran out of time and there was never to be the chance or the moment or the right circumstances to do so.

But in truth I had been hoist with my own petard, for the very strength that I had helped Diana to rally had given her the energy to walk away. I do believe, however, that we have come to a sort of peace and reconciliation now. I felt it during the day of her funeral. As the car bearing her coffin drove slowly through North London I stood with a friend at the edge of a road along which the cortège would pass. Despite the crush, I found myself able, easily, to make my way to the front of the crowd just as the hearse glided in front of me. As I was pushed forward by the crowd and touched the car, I felt also that I touched Diana. I am easier in my thoughts now about our final estrangement.

The summer of 1997 passed, and I was busy enough. Diana needed some rest and hedonistic enjoyment after those two harrowing trips, and I wished her well. Better than most, I knew that she was hurting about Hasnat, so I hadn't been very surprised when she took up with someone else that summer. She had earned a break, and the relationship with Dodi Fayed, which began in July, might have been the perfect summer fling. But if it had indeed been designed to inspire Hasnat's jealousy, I doubt that the tactic worked. If anything, he would have been horrified by the reminder of the depth of public interest in anything she said or did, or anywhere she went, and with whom.

Even now, it amazes me that those few weeks with Dodi—actually only about fourteen days spent together, with a few separations in between—have come to be seen as such an important passage in Diana's life. If she hadn't died at the end of August 1997 I'm convinced that the Dodi episode would be remembered only as a footnote to her life, a simple and sweetly deserved moment of enjoyment, and that by the time autumn passed she would have returned, rested, to her greater purposes, while Dodi would have resolved matters with his fiancée in America. I don't dispute that some spark ignited between them, perhaps something rather more than the impulse that had made Diana want to make Hasnat jealous. Dodi was someone she already knew slightly, he was personable, had a certain position in international society, and was wealthy enough to be able effortlessly to pamper her at a time when she needed not merely to rest, but to be spoiled.

There may have been something subconsciously mischievous about her acceptance of Dodi's largesse and that of his family. In a masterly piece of media manipulation, however, Mohamed al-Fayed appeared, with unreserved approval, to welcome the Princess as close to the bosom of his family as she wished to venture. He, too, considered himself to be a victim of the British Establishment's fixed ideas and prejudices, having been refused citizenship despite the many and profitable enterprises he has sustained in Britain and his avowed loyalty to the Crown. Perhaps he and Diana were simultaneously in a mood to cock a conspiratorial snook. But if so, her agenda was not the same as his.

If Mohamed al-Fayed really thought that Diana and his son were on the brink of announcing their betrothal, then he was the victim of wishful thinking. Diana had her boys and their future to consider and, despite her gradually deepening interest in Middle Eastern matters, was certainly not ready to convert to Islam, as she would have been obliged to do if she had married Dodi. She took a keen interest in all the world's great religions, but that is not the same as taking instruction, nor is it to say that she was about to convert. Her copy of the Koran and her study of its teachings dated back to the most heady times of her passion for Hasnat, when she could not always resist daydreams about a future with him.

That summer, on holiday with Rachel, I took an interest, though not a particularly avid one, in the course of Diana's fling with Dodi as it was reported in newspapers both at home and abroad, thinking it rather funny that this time she was so openly flirtatious in front of the world's paparazzi and seemed to be so relaxed. After all the furtive secrecy with Hasnat, it must have been great fun for her to have a relationship with someone who positively relished public attention. She must also have enjoyed the daylight and open air that had been impossible when she had insisted upon utmost privacy during the courses of earlier affairs. I was sorry that she and I were no longer in touch to talk about it, but was pleased to see her looking so well and cheerful and had little doubt that soon we would be reconciled. All the time in the world to catch up, I thought.

There was so much that I found hard to believe when she died—above all the waste of her. Then came the waves of speculation about engagement rings and last words, conspiracies and recriminations. I could not understand why she was not wearing a safety belt while Trevor Rees-Jones *was* (it is the general practice of bodyguards to sit unencumbered by a seat belt so that they can spring into immediate protective action if necessary). As I sat in frozen disbelief, I found it impossible to imagine what Diana's sons were going through. I dared not even consider what her last seconds must have been like, beyond hoping that she had blanked immediately and knew no pain. I couldn't believe that we hadn't said kind words to each other that last time we spoke, had not even said 'Goodbye' before she died.

Flashes and fragments concerning our last conversations haunted me. Could I actually have climbed down, tried harder to apologize? At least then my memory would not be for ever tarnished with this horrible regret. If Diana hadn't died so utterly unexpectedly all this would seem too preposterous to think about today. In fact, when we'd both calmed down, I know we would have laughed about it. But now there was no time, and there would be no laughter. On one level my grief and disbelief were selfish, concerned with my own pain about the the loss of a friendship once strong enough for Diana herself to describe it as a sort of sisterhood.

At a much more profound level the grief was about the world's loss of such a remarkable woman in the bloom of her recovery, and at the peak of her generosity and gentle powers, a princess who was ready to reach into the very depths of the world's conscience. On that day, however, she opened the world's heart.

We often say that we 'can't believe it' when the enormity of what we know and have experienced—whether joyful or painful—is beyond our usual puny means of expression. And yet we do believe, only too well, that something awesome has happened. I wasn't in denial: of course I believed that Diana was dead. But like millions all over the world, I was in shock on that last black day of August 1997.

Afterword

It's getting on for a year, as I write, since Diana died.

I know that all over the world there are millions of people whose sadness is triggered by the memory of a particular expression, some kind words perhaps addressed uniquely to them as she bent to catch what they were saying or touch their hand. For my part, in the main I feel blessed to have had such a long and enriching friendship with Diana. Enough time has passed for the sharper edges of our last conversations to blur into the wider, softer, brighter memory which remains. For me, certain pieces of music can flick a switch to bring all the joy and poignancy back at once. And when I listen to the same Tchaikovsky ballet music that I once gave her, I know that she's living with the angels now.

So like his mother is he—in ways far transcending the striking physical resemblance—that I'm sure that Prince William will prove to have inherited her innate impulse to use power and position for the greater good. For this reason alone I think he will be a great king. In fact, if he continues his mother's work and maintains both his parents' passionate concern for the care of the disadvantaged, then in that continuation the British monarchy has its best chance of survival. He shows every sign of sharing the Princess's compassionate and egalitarian principles, so that one day William, too, will be ready to say 'Watch out world, here I come.' That, of course, is the saddest of ironies.

I can only hope that Diana's elder son will enjoy a long stretch of relatively calm and normal years before he comes into his awesome destiny. He will be better equipped to deal with it if it is not thrust upon him too soon. And yet it would be a tragedy for him and for the world if he had to wait too long. In this century Britain has already seen two promising heirs to the throne left frustrated and denied as they waited for that call of destiny. Our next monarch should not have to run the risk of squandering his talents and energies before ascending the throne.

In retrospect, I see myself as a companion who joined Diana to walk with her over some of the final miles of an all-too-short journey. When she needed to rest I respected that and when she seemed in danger of stumbling I lent her my hand or shoulder for support. When she needed to digress or detour by herself I was happy to see her test her new strengths, content to wait until she was ready to join me again for another mile or so.

Diana never believed that she would have a long life and often said to me that she would die before her time. 'I know I'll never make old bones,' she said. Part of this was the result of her fatalistic approach to life, but the other part was due to her paranoia. There is an awful irony in the fact that while she died with an Arab, Dodi Fayed, she had for years believed that there was an Arab conspiracy to kill her. She felt that friends of the royal family, notably their rich allies in the Gulf States, would take out a contract on her life. I assured Diana that this was highly unlikely, but in fact there were two men who constantly stalked her, one of them a German. I remember on one occasion we were in the street near Regent's Park and she was being photographed from across the road by her German stalker. He really unnerved her. She lived in a state of agitation, convinced that her phone was bugged, and I remember once, when she was on her mobile phone to me, after thirty minutes of conversation there was a 'beep' on the phone line and Diana said 'Hallo boys [meaning the MI5 listeners], time to change the tape.' In fact, she asked me to contact British Telecom to ask them if my own phone was bugged. They wrote back and duly told me that there was no illegal phone tap on the line, suggesting that I write to the Home Office if I had further complaints. Of course, they never denied, nor could they, that I was being bugged 'officially'. In fact Diana did fear that GCHQ, the government intelligence-gathering organization, was keeping an eye on her. Even when she was driving she would be concerned that the cars behind her were following her. Sometimes it was true, for the paparazzi were following her almost all the time. My own contacts in the security world inform me that if she was being monitored it was simply to protect the children, because she spoke so often about their movements and whereabouts on the telephone that if the information got into the wrong hands they would have been at risk from kidnap attempts or terrorist attacks.

Most people do their growing up when they are children and adolescents, during which time they are under the loving, worried and watchful gaze of parents. They don't have to do so in the full glare of public attention. Considering what she had to endure from cynics, Palace courtiers, supplicants and spongers during those years when we were friends, Diana did her late growing-up with remarkable grace.

How did she grow and change during the years of our friendship? How best do I remember the stages of her journey? In the simplest and most physical sense, Diana became bigger. Her shape altered and assumed healthily womanly proportions as she gained weight. As she grew spiritually she became proud of her height and only stooped if she was deliberately meeting a child or shorter adult eye to eye. She was poised on high heels in public, while there was a different, comfortable assurance as she scuttled about barefoot in her palace home. There were fewer nervous giggles and more throaty laughs. There were no more self-inflicted scratches and lacerations, and as she became mentally and physically stronger she developed faith in her sense of self-worth and purpose. It was an inevitable part of the vital process of becoming less of a shy 'pleaser' that Diana wasn't yet quite strong enough to admit mistakes and apologize as readily as she sometimes might have done. But that graciousness, too, would have come in time.

Important aspects of Diana's life had become simpler, as the numbers of healers and therapists she relied upon lessened. Soon, I believe, she would have largely kicked her most enduring habit—that of colonic irrigation—because there would have been less and less bile to release and ever-widening, better ways to provide the 'high' that those treatments still gave her. Life would have given her better expression, better releases for residual frustrations, so that eventually these frustrations would have been consigned to her past. Already the more Diana studied and experienced the politics of the real world, the less influenced was she by those of the playground.

I think I helped Diana achieve something of all this as I worked with her to strengthen her self-confidence and every aspect of her spiritual growth. I believe my friendship, faith and example helped to convince her that she had exceptional healing powers and I thank God that these were at least used for a little while. My frank approach to Diana may have enabled her, in turn, to be more honest with others than she had been in the past. And this was beginning to enable her to accept constructive, if candid, criticism from other people. She was finding the courage, more and more, to walk ahead steadily without her props. And, sometimes, to let go.

Of the many images of Diana that I retain one recurs exceptionally often. It isn't *quite* one of a princess in disguise, for in this memory she employs no subterfuge or protection other than that of her own aura. But that aura was very strong, and did indeed guard her—and she did need that protection. I am not speaking here of Diana's fearless strides across fields known to be studded with anti-personnel landmines, but of another risk she frequently took, against my advice.

Late at night at Kensington Palace, when I was tired and ready to go home, a barefooted Diana would sometimes come and stand outside the palace with me and wait until the cab arrived. She'd have changed into sweats and placed a band around her forehead, and after waving me away she would then pull on her trainers and, restless and driven but cheerful, would run confidently through the quiet, dark streets of Knightsbridge and Kensington. She set off with a calm sense of purpose, presumably gathering speed as she ran alone through those dim night streets. And presumably protected as she fixed her course, eventually to return to the quiet safety of the place where she was at home, although alone.

I needn't have worried then. Some star was watching and guiding her, protecting the brave, self-testing and solitary Diana. That star may, indeed, have rendered her invisible to whatever dangers waited in the dark. How ironic it was, then, that the Princess met her death at a moment when she might well have assumed that she was safer and better cared for than ever before in her troubled, often fractured, but glorious life.

No nonsense about Diana the Huntress here. For herself, she sought little more than what she already had. Whatever clothes and jewels she wore, whatever little-girl games she sometimes played, and however skilfully she might at times disguise herself, Diana, to me, will always look like that brave and naked-faced young woman who ran with strength and optimism into the night—and back towards a place she called home because her sons did so too.

We all know how the world was diminished by Diana's death. We, and future generations, have yet to learn how it was enriched by her life.

APPENDIX

On Being a Healer

I 'saw' things as a child—people and animals which weren't physically there—but I don't think this is particularly unusual. Many children have extraordinary perceptive abilities, and at least I was not ridiculed or punished for mentioning mine. Perhaps I was a singular child, however, for I'm told that I was speaking at eight months although, curiously, I didn't walk until I was two. It may be that my energies were expressed very early on in the emotional and creative, rather than physical, side of life.

As I grew up I excelled at piano lessons, so that my father hoped I might become a concert pianist; sadly, however, my hands were too small for this idea ever to be developed. Again, although I was thought to be exceptionally talented at art at school I think my parents, loving as they were, but strictly conventional in their attitudes towards us, worried that art school would fill my head with too many dangerous, hippy ideas, so I lost that little fight. This was in the early 1970s when most parents still assumed that their daughters would be married and settled within a few years of leaving school, so what was the point of further education? Perhaps, too, some of my teen-aged attempts at rebellion may have made them especially

207

cautious, for I was constantly breaking the school's petty little rules in my own limited ways.

Neither I nor either of my sisters was especially nurtured intellectually. Juliette, my slightly younger sister, joined me at the local grammar school, but Rachel, who, although also bright, was not academically gifted, went to a different school. With that over, Rachel worked as a professional hair stylist until the terrible accident splintered her life, and Juliette worked in an office before marrying Russell, a brilliant young entrepreneur who, with my father's help, went on to build the Café Flo chain of brasseries and now has Giraffe Cafés. Juliette, always something of an energy hurricane, was certainly his powerful, steering influence. Conversely, I searched for years before I found my true path.

As I have said, what set me on that path was my experience during and after Rachel's long recovery. Now, although she will always have residual problems, she drives, travels, sometimes cuts peoples' hair, squabbles and picnics. Not quite like a normal person, but as a *special*, singular and unique person. Her own. She has taught me so much. Today, with little power of memory, she has no choice but to live in the here and now and that is what I have, consequently, learned to do.

Misfortune, tragedy even, can so often be the wisest teacher. Our mother has been ill for some years and was not expected to last long when her cancer was identified in 1994. Yet the fact that several years later she remains feisty and independent may in some way be related to the ways that I have tried to help her, including positive thoughts, absent healing, and the lessons about positive aura which I learned from Rachel.

Auras are both simple and complicated, which makes

them difficult to explain, particularly as the word has become overused, and sometimes misused, to describe things like sex appeal, business power, evil qualities, or charisma. The fact is that we all have an energy spirit power which is not visible to the naked eye, and however we might try, we cannot control the electromagnetic emanations. Two Russian scientists, Semyan D. and Valentina K. Kirlian, were able to capture these human auras on film in a technique which has become known as Kirlian photography. In such photographs waves of colour can be seen surrounding a human body, and these colours change according to the person's mood or state of health. However, I don't use or need photographs of these auras as I work—I *know* they are there.

I work through the aura from inside to the outer, physical, layers, correcting imbalances, removing negative influences, and then I try to realign a client's balance by healing cracks in their aura, dealing with their fears and clearing out blockages. Precise details of my work are hard to give as things will vary from client to client and in any case—by their very nature—do not translate well to the bald sterility of the page. For any client wanting detailed information on how healing works, I recommend the healing 'bible', *Hands of Light* by Barbara Ann Brennan (I don't have one myself), so unlike some healers I do not claim any unique power or method.

After a session or series of sessions clients are often light-headed and feel sufficiently unburdened, both mentally and physically, as to be empowered to take control of their own lives. When that stage is reached we usually part company—my work is done.

Since it seems that my mission is to heal, I am more concerned with damaged auras than healthy ones, and I know now that I can advise people who are suffering and in pain. Once I identify the damage I can suggest practical solutions for physical problems—perhaps by recommending some other specialist healer or doctor, or by discussing spiritual, emotional or psychological difficulties with the client. I am not a doctor, nor have I any formal scientific training. The success of my work depends on faith and trust and I never venture outside my field of influence or ability, but over and over again I have guided people towards the right specialist for *their* unique dilemma. Just as I 'saw' as a child, I can now see what help my clients really need and help them to seize back control of their lives.

I have held my hands near clients and seen potential cancers in their auras and then offered guidance. Many cancers are rooted in emotional trauma or shock, frequently compounded by stress. It has often been that stress, compounded with emotional trauma, which I have observed and been able to correct, or help to correct, by means of skills I have acquired but which I still do not fully understand. In other cases I can advise as to what treatment the client might best consider next, whether it is acupuncture, homeopathic attention, a changed diet or conventional surgery or medicine, even though many clients might have become wary of these last options.

I do *know* that, unlike many healers, I can see the whole spiritual, emotional, physical and psychological picture at once—all contained within the waves that I see and feel when I work with a client. Sometimes, in helping them, I absorb their pain. This is not something I welcome but I regard it as part of my job and it is up to me to deal with it. Often this means periods of rest and psychic cleansing to rid myself of negative energies that I may have absorbed from my clients as they release them. Once or twice I have had to decide to turn a potential client away: if I have a strong sense that the person—perhaps a schizophrenic on strong medication—is going to tire and damage me, I have to be firm, however much pity and concern I may feel.

So dealing with stresses and potential cancers is central to my work. When I see that I have corrected a damaged aura by removing negative energies I know that my work is, not completed, but accomplished. Sometimes, not always, I can do more, for I have also come to accept my powers of 'absent healing', by which I mean that even if the suffering person is not physically with me I can send them waves of healing energy. I have the word of many that this works; indeed, it can be the most effective healing that I offer.

I only speak of possible trouble ahead if I'm pretty sure that the client can cope with such news or will accept advice from me or from some other specialist that I might recommend. At times I am rather frightened of the gift/ power/curse—call it what you will—that was bestowed on me. I am well aware that clients have assured me that through my work and advice ulcers have disappeared, varicose veins have shrunk, melanomas have retreated, and so on. But while this is all very heartening, it is scary too. In some ways I feel more confident about my healing when I'm dealing with an emotional problem, although, naturally, I recognize that physical and emotional problems are often connected.

Sometimes having the power to predict things can be less of a blessing than a curse. On the day in May 1996 that my father died of a massive heart attack I had a cold and frightening certainty that there would be a death in my family home. Actually, I thought that it was my mother who was fated, and became so convinced of impending disaster that I called her sister back from a holiday in Holland. But it was Dad, apparently much fitter than average for a man of seventy, who died within hours of his collapse. There had been no warning—he had been enjoying life to the full right until the moment of his attack.

I never need to read or tune into the weather forecast. I can feel, sometimes with physical pain, if we are in for storms or snow or great heat. More importantly, perhaps, I've noticed that people who seek me out for healing will often ask me about threatening events in the future, and are usually less interested in the happy things that might well lie ahead. I suppose it is human nature for people to want to confront the bleak side of what may come and thereby anticipate ways of limiting the damage. Diana did this, in a way, when she read her runes or consulted astrologers, as she did at least once a fortnight. She only went to experts like the justly celebrated Debbie Frank, scorning newspaper and magazine astrologers, rightly, as not being personal enough. She hugged happy predictions to herself as if grasping at straws, yet if she received bad news she would appear to dismiss that with a giggle, too. In reality, she stored the information away and would regurgitate it, endlessly analysing it, if misfortune did later strike.

I'm far from cynical where astrology is concerned, but it does sometimes amuse me how people who have such deep faith in their chosen seers' powers seldom lose that trust when predicted horrors *don't* come to pass. Perhaps this rather uncritical trust is rooted in relief that disaster foretold has been avoided by mysterious and unforeseeable planetary movements. Perhaps it is the result of gratitude towards a trusted astrologer whose influence may have helped to avert this heavenly clash. But whatever the reason, astrologers seem to have it both ways. Diana's dependency on astrology and psychics tended to display the same unquestioning faith. In early 1995, for example, she was plunged into a state of panic when it was predicted to her that the Queen would die that November. Formally separated, but not yet divorced from Prince Charles, Diana's dismay was rooted in a combination of concern for her monarch, anxiety about how the Prince would cope with his mother's death, and an understandably selfish worry about how such a turn of events would affect her at that crucial stage. Could she, technically, become Queen? Would the divorce proceedings be put on indefinite hold? To a cynical outsider Diana's anxieties may have appeared laughable, but all these fears were very real to her and she was heady with relief as November passed without this ultimate and potentially disastrous complication. This did not, however, stop her from continuing to visit astrologers and psychics.

Over the years that I knew her, Diana had become ever more observant of and eager to learn about my way of healing. So enthused was she about the positive effects of some healings and therapies, and so confident—rightly— of her own power to bestow relief through touch and spiritual guidance, that by early 1995 she believed she could cut across or circumvent the years of practice, of tentative help offered informally to clients, that most healers go through as a kind of apprenticeship. In short, she lacked not only practice, but also many of the vital complementary skills with which any healer worthy of the name has to be equipped.

That she had a gift is unquestionable, however. Liz Tilberis, the British editor of American *Harper's & Queen*, who was friendly with Diana, has said that when she was threatened by ovarian cancer at around this time, she received great strength from Diana, 'a feeling of pure light' reaching her during telephone conversations. She attributes a significant part of her recovery to the waves of healing and positive energy that the Princess sent her. By 1996, since some of Diana's tension, her paranoia, her phobias and depression had lifted, she was ready to help other people as well as deal with her own practical and legal stresses. Furthermore, since she now had concrete dilemmas to address she was much less prone to being engulfed by irrational glooms. Even while proceedings ground on, she was able to cope astonishingly well with the divorce worries and still have time to care for others. Meetings at the lawyers' offices or at KP, which might have exhausted her before, she was able to take in her stride.

How will I ever forget that dreadful day in 1996, over two years after I had first met Diana, when my father died, my mother was in hospital, and I wrecked my car in a stupid crash on my way home? I'm amazed both that I was allowed to drive at all after dealing with all that and that I suffered no more than whiplash injuries, a big bump on my forehead and severe cuts on my legs. Bereaved, injured and trapped in a surgical collar, I didn't think that I could work again. Diana helped me through this, gave me the strength to return to work.

Cynics might suggest that this desire to heal, which produced in her a determination to learn from me how to harness her own healing power, was another form of therapy, that it was thus selfish in some way. And yet the same could be said of anyone whose life is centred upon the well-being of others. It may have given Diana some satisfaction to bury and lose herself in other people's griefs, but her concern was not only driven by a wish to avoid confronting her own miseries. She genuinely cared about others, and was thrilled when she found that she could be of help and use. In any case, Diana wasn't a saint: she was perfectly capable of acts of self-interest as well as of altruism, and there was no mistaking or disguising the former when she had placed herself at the top of her own agenda. Those were the times when her most compelling interest and hobby—*herself*—came to the fore, and when she would have not hesitated to adopt the small self-indulgence of calling friends at all times of the day or night, believing, usually with justification, that she had the right to expect that trusted people would always be there for her.

She gave enough time, interest and effort to other people for this to be forgiven. Given that she did not have the kind of sporting, cultural or practical interests that many people escape into when they need to relax, it was some time before Diana began to discourage the countless therapists, gurus and commentators whose attentions suggested to her that she was worthy of infinite scrutiny. She had been *encouraged* to become self-obsessed. By late 1996 she was becoming confident that she did indeed possess the healing powers the media attributed to her every time she was filmed or photographed tending someone sick or dispossessed.

It is easily understood. She gave out waves of compassion on every visit, with every hug. With every reciprocal wave of love—even the sight of her, let alone her touch, was enough, briefly, to make many of the sick feel stronger, the abandoned rescued and the hopeless cherished—she felt she had received more strength to give back to the disadvantaged. She had no messianic delusions, no thought of miraculously raising a latter-day Lazarus, but as early as spring 1996 Diana was keen to reach to the limits of her healing strengths. What had begun as informed curiosity during our earliest evenings at Kensington Palace steadily became more of a preoccupation. As I have said, she had asked Mother Teresa if she could come to her mission in Calcutta to offer help. The offer was declined, gently, on the grounds that the missionary felt that Diana was still too troubled herself to be able to give much to others. Disappointed but undeterred, Diana strove to harness her strengths and was desperate to learn how best to do so. She read voraciously on the subject, asked me about everything I knew. By late 1996 she had definitely decided that she could be a healer in some more formalized way than simply giving hope and strength through her presence. It was a job she felt she was born to.

I was fairly uneasy about Diana's interest in healing at first, but did not know how to make her pace herself. She was impressed by what I had helped her to achieve and she longed to heal others in turn, using my methods of concentration, touch and the drawing down of energies into the hands and fingertips and thence into the suffering core of someone else. She was convinced that dealing with her own pain had given her the capacity to become an empowerer. All her sorrows—that of her marriage, her important but failed love affair, and the, to her, equally important but disastrously misjudged ro-

mantic friendship, the death of her father, unresolved dis-
cord between her and other members of her family—and
her proven ability to survive all this, supported Diana's
conviction that she could heal others of their pain.

How could I disagree? When she had given me such
strong waves of restorative help after my father died, I
had recognized that she could become a natural healer
and I wanted to encourage her. But as early as 1995,
when I had told her that she had to recover a little more
herself before she could give her best to others, she was
impatient and dismayed, unwilling to accept that we
should proceed a little more slowly. Her eagerness was
touching. Any teacher wants to encourage a willing
pupil, and thus tends to be ambivalent about almost
scolding her over wanting to run before she can walk. In
Diana's case, this meant insisting that she deal with her
own problems before she attempted to solve those of
others. But Diana was so pleased to hear that she had the
potential to heal that she couldn't wait to test her
powers, her ability to channel energies. She had such a
great need to be needed, and I was well aware that if she
successfully helped others she would, in turn, be helped,
something that remained my principal wish and concern.

Even so, she still had to learn how to differentiate between a person's vital need to be accepted by their peers
and the other human need for a more private, unconditional love of the type she'd hoped to find within her
marriage. I tried to show her that although she might
often help other people with the former it was unrealistic
for her to set herself up as someone who could always
offer the latter. Sincere depths of care, concern and genuine affection may be offered universally, but the sort of
love she had for her sons and a very few other special

people in her life could not be given to everyone. But even understanding that reality did not diminish the level of Diana's genuine compassion for the great mass of ordinary people, and she was always in danger of asking too much of herself. It would have been impossible for her personally to show her care to every suffering person in the world. None the less, Diana stretched herself as far as a person could once she became convinced that she had exceptional healing strength to bestow as richly and widely as possible.

Through me she learned about light energy. I had told her of the white-gold light I saw in her aura and felt to emanate from her, particularly when she prayed for special strength or courage in order to help those less fortunate, or when she was preparing herself to walk through the minefields in Angola. Tense times with Hasnat made her aura a dirty brownish-grey. Her stresses, fears and emotional pains would most often be expressed in back and shoulder aches and agonizing knots in the stomach.

Just as everyone has their own pain threshold, each individual will emit their own colours and vibrations, depending on the emotional, physical or psychological state they are in. It is my job to 'read' these colours and to offer healing accordingly. Diana had much to learn yet about these skills. She had great strength, certainly, and definitely, with time, had come to learn how to connect with it, focus it and use it effectively through touch, voice and gaze. But she had many internal quandaries to resolve before she could have offered her best as a healer of others. I believe that anyone can heal but the individual must be reasonably well focused and balanced themselves before they are ready or able to do much for others. The whole point is to empower the client and create or re-create a sense of responsibility for self. With sufficient motivation that person will ultimately be able to step forward alone and recapture the power to control their own body and life.

My way of healing does not involve painful injections, unsettling drugs or traumatizing surgery, but I had told Diana that someone with a basic but untrained gift could not simply plunge into the field and at once begin to work effectively. As I've said, she was certainly eager to learn— but perhaps not in quite the right way, not yet. She was still seeing a number of therapists right up to the summer before her death. I don't flatter or delude myself, and think it likely that she was attempting to learn from them as diligently as she listened to and absorbed whatever knowledge I could impart. Sometimes, however, too much information can confuse rather than clarify, as anyone who has ever struggled to understand a computer manual or to register the complexities embedded in the small print of an insurance policy will testify. Diana wanted to learn so much, so fast and some of the information she was absorbing needed to be considered and refined. She really wasn't ready to offer clearly thought-out healing.

Nevertheless, under my guidance she began to understand about the power of sunlight. I would ask her to visualize and try to feel that lovely bright and healing warmth enter her body through the top of her head and then to feel it sink through her feet into the ground where stresses would be discharged. When she was cleansed, released and ready I would suggest that she then allowed that force to stretch down her arms and reach her fingertips. With that healing power flooding through her hands Diana could and did begin to offer restorative touches and hugs to other people.

I've tried here to simplify what is in fact a complex subject. It was actually quite a lot to learn and, as I say, Diana was certainly building up knowledge from elsewhere as well. But she was not, in my opinion, anywhere near ready to act as the fully fledged healer she wished to be, and finally was by the end of 1996. By March 1997 she was ready to fly.

I do believe that what goes around comes around again, and in benign chance, in good turns being repaid and good luck being recycled. I suppose I approach my healing work with something of the same optimism. Extraordinary surprises, miracles even, are possible. We humans can gather together the necessary nerve and faith, and sometimes this is rewarded by luck—fortune, they say, favours the brave. I sometimes struggle to cling to these beliefs in the wake of Diana's death, but somehow I believe that the tragedy will prove to be as valuable as her life, that future generations all over the world will lead safer, richer lives because of her.

Index

221